SCENI
WEST CORK

Damien Enright is a journalist, television writer, presenter and broadcaster. He has written a weekly nature column in the *Irish Examiner* since 1990, contributed articles to *Walking World Ireland* magazine, presented *Enright's Way*, a three-part series for RTÉ television, and is the author of eight popular walking guides to West Cork and Kerry. His critically acclaimed *A Place Near Heaven: A Year in West Cork* was published in 2004.

www.damienenright.com

The moment my legs begin to move, my thoughts begin to flow . . .

Henry David Thoreau (1817–1862)

Sherkin Friary

SCENIC WALKS IN WEST CORK

A Walking Guide

Damien Enright

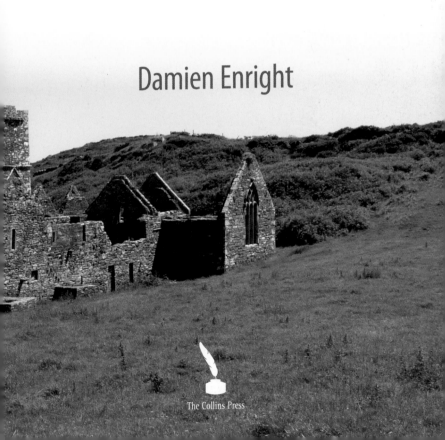

The Collins Press

First published in 2011 by
The Collins Press
West Link Park
Doughcloyne
Wilton
Cork

Reprinted 2013

All photographs courtesy of the author

British Library Cataloguing in Publication Data
Enright, Damien.
Scenic walks in West Cork : a walking guide.
1. Walking—Ireland—Cork (County)—Guidebooks.
2. Cork (Ireland : County)—Guidebooks.
I. Title
796.5'1'094195-dc22

ISBN: 978-184889-104-3

Design and typesetting by Fairways Design

Typeset in Avenir

Printed in Poland by Drukarnia Skleniarz

Contents

Bantry and Castletownbere

Ferry and Cable-car Timetables

Old lighthouse and Napoleonic signal tower, Cape Clear Island

Introduction

The compilation of this book owes much to my wife, Marie. While she checked the hard facts of the routes and the maps, I strolled along in another world, talking to myself on a recording machine, stopping to explore nature, human history or prehistory, and to photograph vistas, flowers or frogs. Often, I would have been lost without her. Meanwhile, we shared, in the case of each and every round, our admiration of the Irish countryside and the joy of walking it together.

Many of us enjoy walking in company but my company, I sometimes think, might enjoy the walk better without me. I constantly lag behind – and then huff and puff to try to catch up while they, the walker-walkers, the dedicated single-minded walkers, have to pause and wait for me. But there is much the busy walker misses in passing. When I see folk route-marching along, arms flying, mini-headphones in their ears, I sometimes think they should stay at home and watch nature programmes on television while using one of those conveyor-belt walking machines.

I am not of the single-minded walker stripe: I have many things on my mind besides putting one foot in front of the other at a hectic pace. I am intrigued with what I see – there is *always* something to see: it may be a historic ruin or, simply, a roadside wall interesting because of the distinctive and beautiful way the stones have been laid, and because of the array of plants colonising them. It may be a wayside flower, or a strange bug, the light reflecting on ivy leaves in a dark forest or small trout darting in the flow of a brown river. It may be a toadstool scored with tiny tooth marks – a wood mouse or, possibly, a bank vole, a relatively recent emigrant to Ireland. Those 'toadstools', so called, may on closer inspection be identified as wood blewitts or chanterelles and make a fine meal. Meanwhile, is that bushel of twigs high up in the tree a magpie's domed nest or a red squirrel's drey? There is more to walking than exercise. There is a universe to explore and it changes with each passing season, each passing week and passing day.

I stop and stare and wonder about things. At home, I take out books and look them up. I learn constantly. I am a perambulating hedge scholar. The walks I have written about herein are generally short but one may take hours over them. The commentaries are for those who, like myself, stop and look closely, or peer into the distance. Which islands are those we can see now, of the hundred islands and islets of Roaringwater Bay?

JAMES FORT WALK

Key points: Duggan Bridge – Castle Park – James Fort – Ringrone – Sandy Cove – Ballymacaw Cross

Start/finish: the Dock Pub in Castlepark at the opposite side of the Duggan Bridge from Kinsale town, about 3.2km (2 miles) west of the town centre, grid ref.: W644495

Distance: (A) 3.2km (2 miles); (B) 8km (5 miles)
Map: OSi Sheet 87 **Walking Time:** including viewing the fort
(A) 1 hour 30 minutes, (B) 3 hours

Route A

(1) The Dock Pub. We pass the pub and the landing place for a cross-harbour ferry before the bridge was built. At the time of the Battle of Kinsale, 1601, there was a boatyard here. Great beams of iroko – ironwood – probably used to support boats during repairs, were recovered in recent times.

With the marina on our left, we pass the Marina Office and turn right at the gable of the last house in the row, Ferry House, along a narrow path between it and a roofless barn. After climbing a few stone steps, we reach a pathway and turn left. The pathway climbs a little at first and crosses a stile to a fingerpost indicating James Fort. The path is easy, with excellent views over the mouth of the Bandon River. The country is wild, with gorse, bracken and heather. Across the water is Kinsale, two small piers with fishing boats immediately opposite and a line of tiny 'toy town' cottages above. Higher still are some fine Georgian houses in stately gardens. Farther along is the main Kinsale marina, with the town rising behind, a very beautiful town with tall buildings climbing the hill and, off to the right, before Scilly woods, a line of apartment blocks, known locally as the Cash Registers for their resemblance to same and the profits they have engendered.

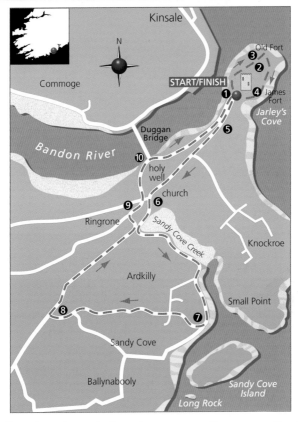

All efforts by paint and plantation to camouflage or ameliorate their presence have so far proved unsuccessful.

Along the pathway, the stone wall is grown over with dark green navelwort. Herb Robert, with bright red stalks and dark green leaves, is also abundant. Also, there is hart's-tongue fern, shiny green and like the long, pointed tongue of a hart, or deer, and hard fern, and spleenwort and wall rue. With yellow and grey lichens, primroses, violets, foxgloves, montbretia and garlic-smelling ransoms, the walls along this walk are a potpourri of smells and colours in spring and summer.

(2) To our right, now, are the ramparts of James Fort. One may climb these now – they are more like earth mounds than walls – or enter, later, by a gate known as the Drawbridge, which we will pass on the south side. A platform, along which sentries might patrol, runs all around the top of the ramparts and so makes a tour a relatively easy matter. The views are wonderful, with Kinsale to the north, the pretty village of Summer Cove and monolithic Charles Fort due east across the harbour, the opening to the sea southwards, and the broad meanders of the River Bandon to the west.

James Fort was begun in 1602, a year after the Battle of Kinsale, at the expense of the townspeople in return for the restoration of the town's charter. The cost was not only a 'fine' imposed on them for their collusion with the Spaniards, but also ensured that protection against any future Catholic 'invasion' was paid for by the Irish themselves. Strategically, the site was perfect, overlooking the harbour mouth and on high ground almost surrounded by water but for the narrow isthmus at the Dock bar. Built on the site of the earlier 'Chastell Parke' – which had been occupied by the Spaniards in 1601 – the construction was 'state-of-the-art' for the times with, probably, the first use of bastions in Irish fortification.

Passing the fort on the right, we enter a large green field with a ruined house at the end. It is worth pausing at this ruin – once a billet for soldiers manning the defences below – to enjoy the magnificent view. Below, the land falls sharply away to a stone fort, the Blockhouse, on the edge of the water. The path that leads down to it – around the ruin's gable – was high-ditched to protect soldiers going back and

James Fort

The Blockhouse with Summer Cove opposite

forth to the Blockhouse. It slopes steeply and can be slippery in wet weather, like a muddy Cresta Run. Reasonable caution is required to avoid tobogganing into the building below.

(3) The Blockhouse, built long before the fort, in 1549, allowed emplaced cannon to rake the channel at point-blank range. From here, a defensive iron chain was sometimes floated to the other shore, barring entry to the harbour at night or in times of danger. The floor is of bedrock, and the stone structure is roughly semicircular. The arched windows, latticed with iron bars, look across at colourful Summer Cove and the massive grey bulk of Charles Fort, rising out of the sea.

Emerging, and before retracing one's steps, with some effort, up the 'Cresta Run', it is worth climbing the scalp of bare rock immediately to the left and enjoying the fine view down the coastline between the headlands of the bay. Having trudged up the path which we slithered down, we pass the ruin again on our right and continue towards some other ruins straight ahead; these are the remains of the inner fort of James Fort.

Stonechats are common here, standing prominently on briars or fence wires to sing. The call is said to resemble two pebbles struck together, hence the name. Yellowhammers may also be seen, the cocks as bright as canaries. With luck, one may spot a merlin – which eats yellowhammers – scudding low over the heath land, fast as a fleeting shadow, glimpsed and then gone. The wall beside the pathway is rich in mosses and wayside plants, especially foxgloves, tall stalks of purple flowers, many fingers and no thumbs.

(4) Now reaching again the ramparts of James Fort, the path divides into three, to right and left following the dry moat outside the ramparts and, in the centre, climbing the ramparts. The centre path takes us to the ruins, with stone buildings, as mentioned in (2), above. We enter and explore the ruins and, then, with the ruins on our right, pass, via the Drawbridge, a stone-faced cutting through the ramparts, to the moat outside. To the left, a bastion riddled with rabbit burrows blocks our way: we go right, following the moat and climb via a gap in the wall to a path outside the structure. This leads back to the Dock and Castle Park, following a well-worn path that diverges from the ramparts and descends diagonally across the field towards a line of evergreen 'palms', so-called locally because the leaves are blessed in the church on Palm Sundays. Just before the sea, the path turns right through a stile and leads onto a small beach, Jarley's Cove. We cross the top of this pleasant beach – the lawn that abuts it is marked

Jarley's Cove

Bandon River and Duggan Bridge

'Private Garden' – and exit on the other side, where we follow a path between hedges returning us in front of the Dock bar. We have now completed Route A.

Route B

(5) The road leading away from the Dock bar forks. We go left, climbing up the hill. There are good views of the escarpment opposite, and the fine houses on its slopes. This road ascends gradually, but steadily, to high ground with extensive views over the mouth of the Bandon River and the 'new' Duggan Bridge.

Ignoring a road to the left, we continue to the top, where a path through a graveyard on the right of the road leads to the ruined church of Courtmaher, the 'mother church'. While closely connected with the Norman family, De Courcy – Myles De Courcy was first Baron of Kinsale in 1223 – local lore holds that St Patrick departed from here

Sandycove and The Pill

to visit Rome and, indeed, that there was a church near here that pre-dated St Patrick. Little now remains of Courtmaher but the ruins, with the De Courcy castle of Ringrone reduced to a single stalwart gable standing in the nearby field.

(6) Returning to the road, we go right and descend steeply to a signpost indicating 'Sandy Cove I mile'. We follow the sign and do not turn right uphill, but go straight ahead, down to the shores of a small inlet, Sandy Cove Creek. Here, a stone bridge crosses the creek at a hairpin bend. This creek is full of sand gobies, small plaice and small eels. Kingfishers are resident here and, with luck, we may see one fishing from a perch protruding above the water.

The road now follows the southern shore of the inlet, with the water on the left, to the small hamlet of Sandy Cove. This, with flowering blackthorn in spring or orange montbretia and sweet-smelling honeysuckle in summer is a pleasant rural walk, with a tang of the sea. Soon after the Pill, a small island across the channel from the village, comes into view, a road climbs steeply to the right. We will be taking this road, but might first like to explore the pleasant little settlement just a few hundred metres along. Swimming to the island is popular with local youth. The island is the home of a herd of wild goats, beloved of Sandy Cove residents. A cliffside walk extends to an old chapel, Court a Phorteen, (Church of the Little Harbour), beyond the village but does not make a 'round'.

(7) The road we take is to the right just before the hamlet. It initially turns back on itself and then rises steeply, with magnificent views down the coast, past Hake Head to the Old Head of Kinsale. In the distance, there appear to be two hazy headlands, each with a 'tower'. In fact, both promontories are part of the Old Head, the nearer building being one of the line of coastal signal towers built to guard against a French invasion, c. 1796, and the farther, 6.5km (4 miles) away, the lighthouse at the tip. The Old Head is steeped in history, prehistory and legend, and was a naturalist's paradise until it was extensively developed as a private golf course in the mid-1990s.

(8) Reaching a T-junction at Ballymacaw Cross Roads, we turn right. The road soon begins to descend steeply, with the land falling away to the left and the R600 road on the opposite side of the valley. Honeysuckle drapes the trees that form a tunnel around us as we go steeply downhill towards the creek below. Arriving at the headwaters of the creek, we go straight ahead and now must retrace our earlier route for a few hundred metres.

(9) At the Sandy Cove signpost we passed earlier, we go right uphill. Here, we immediately meet the main road, the R600, and turn right towards Kinsale. This is an awkward stretch of road when there is heavy traffic – however, we soon leave it. (Walkers who would prefer a quieter route should return to the Dock via the high road we walked previously). The stump of Ringrone stands high above the slope overgrown with gorse, brambles and the white, trumpet-like flowers of bindweed. Below us, on the left, is the Bandon River.

(10) We shortly pass the southern end of Duggan Bridge and continue straight ahead down the bay-side road which, after about 1km (0.5 miles), will bring us to the Dock Pub and our starting point.

SCILLY AND
CHARLES FORT WALK

Key points: the east shore of Kinsale Harbour – Lower Road
and Scilly Walk – Summer Cove – Charles Fort – Charles Fort
Walk option – Ringacurra – High Road – Breakheart Hill

Start/finish: Scilly Well, Kinsale, grid ref.: W644505

Distance: 6.5 km (4 miles) plus 3.2km (2 miles) option.
Map: OSi Sheet 87
Walking Time: 2 hours, plus an hour at
Charles Fort and a further 1-hour option

To reach the start point at Scilly Well, leave the Post Office in the centre of Kinsale town and follow the pavement to the left; pass the supermarket and walk under the decorative iron balconies of the Perryville House Hotel. The road divides at a Y-junction. Take the lower road, following the water. There is good car parking just before Scilly Well, which is located at the hairpin bend where the road turns right and climbs. On the corner, there is a green space, and a spring. Here, we begin the walk.

(1) Behind Scilly Well, a path leads into Deasy's Bog, wet ground earmarked as a wildlife park, with a footworn track for a short distance. A signpost announces 'Featherbed Lane' and 'Breakheart Hill'; we will be returning via the latter and the story behind these names can then be told. Meanwhile, we round the hairpin and begin the gentle climb up the pavement on the left side of the road. We pass a small garden, with seats and a limestone block carved with the word 'Scilly'. This, the name of the area, may come from the Irish word for the flexible sally branches used in the construction of lobster pots. A more imaginative, or silly, proposition is that it was the home of a colony of refugee smugglers from the Scilly Isles.

We continue along the gable of The Spaniards Inn. Kinsale quite legitimately makes much of its connection with Spain. On 2 October

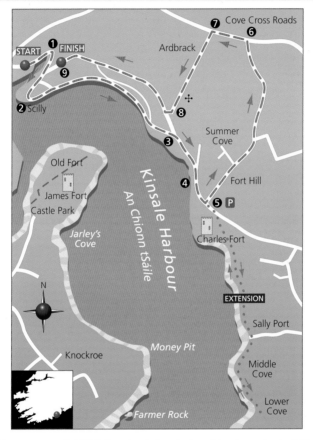

1601, an army of 4,000 Spaniards landed and took control of Kinsale, Castle Park and Ringrone (see Brown's Mills walk). In November, an English force of 7,500 besieged them in the town. In December, a large Irish force under O'Neill and O'Donnell of Ulster marched the length of Ireland in atrocious weather and deployed behind the English lines. Despite the advantage of greater numbers, the Irish and Spanish were defeated. The Battle of Kinsale signalled the end of the old Irish world, of the Gaelic lordships, and a distinctive way of life.

As we come to The Spaniards corner, we do not round it but continue straight across, down a road descending to the water, affording views of the terraced town, the grey bulk of the Mercy Convent pre-eminent. At the water, there is a boat slip, piled with lobster pots and ropes; in the past, Scilly was a fishing community, and small-boat fishermen still moor here.

(2) The narrow street turns left and we pass The Spinnaker public house. Across the water, Castle Park 'island' is in clear view, with James Fort, the ruined soldiers' quarters and the Blockhouse. Meanwhile, the terrestrial view ahead is the shocking pinks, pastel greens and powder blues of the Ardbrack Heights apartment blocks, otherwise known as the Cash Registers (see James Fort Walk). In contrast, we may wish to rest our eyes on the lovely yellow house deep in the woods ahead, or the pier and stately frontages of Summer Cove, or the great, grey ramparts of Charles Fort, rising above the sea.

A road arrives from the left and, now, a terrace of small houses face one another on either side of our route. We pass a sign saying 'Cul de sac'. Steps lead down to the weedy shore.

The narrow roadway runs alongside, and 6m (20 feet) above, the water. After 135m (150 yards), a wicket on the left accesses a leafy pathway to the road above. We continue along the water, passing some seats and a colourful ancient pump on our right. The mouth of

Castle Park across Kinsale Harbour, seen from Scilly

The Blockhouse on Castle Park, seen from Scilly

the harbour comes into view, then the open sea and, in the opposite direction, Duggan Bridge and the Bandon River.

This is a lovely, leafy walk. Three-cornered garlic bedecks the ditches on the left. Farther along, a substantial grove, including Monterey Cypresses (Macrocarpa) climbs the slopes to the left (I once saw a long-eared owl here) before we pass the yellow house amongst trees; the path runs in front of and below it. The path shortly veers slightly left and climbs to the tarred road just above the village of Summer Cove.

(3) The walk downhill to Summer Cove is narrow with small, pretty houses, brightly painted, on either side. While a comparison with Cornish villages or seafront hamlets like Dylan Thomas' village in *Under Milk Wood* may be made, this street has a Spanish Galician flavour.

At sea level, we have a boat slip and the Bulman pub, called after a rock off the east shore and a buoy hung with bells that tolled a warning when the sea got rough. A car park now occupies what was once a quay. We face a steep, but very short, climb out of the village and up the hill ahead.

(4) Fort Hill is steep, but well worth it. Reaching the flat summit, we have top-of-the-world views over the harbour mouth, the Atlantic, the Old Head of Kinsale and Bream Rock. Charles Fort is open to

Charles Fort with Castle Park and the Blockhouse across the harbour

the public from mid-April to October, with an exhibition and guided tours.

The fort is a like a huge block of sharp-cornered stone, stolid, squat, apparently impregnable, at least from the sea where it rises from the shoreline rocks in massive bulwarks and bastions. A 'five-pointed bastion fort', it was built in 1680 as part of the elaborate defences of the town, nervous of a sea attack by Louis XIV of France. It is considered one of the finest examples surviving. The name was changed from Ringcurran to Charles Fort by the British, in honour of King Charles II of England, first proclaimed at St Multose Church, Kinsale, in 1649. It was attacked from land by William of Orange's generals in 1690, the moat on the landward side providing no defence against guns on the higher ground above. Over the centuries, Kinsale was an important Royal Navy base and the fortress continued in use by British forces until 1921.

At the far end of the iron railings along the car park outside Charles Fort, we can take an unpaved track running down towards

Charles Fort, seen from Castle Park

the sea. This will join a recently made gravelled path which runs along the bay side passing Middle Cove to Lower Cove, which will be reached in about 20 minutes. It is a there-and-back spur off the main itinerary, but well worth walking if one has time. Initially, we pass an old cemetery outside the fort walls, and then cross a stream beside a small, gravelled beach, Sally Fort. Wayside plaques provide a historical commentary. There is a right-of-way path, clearly marked, through the Kinsale Boatyard at Middle Cove.

(5) The main route of our walk, however, takes the road signposted 'Kinsale and Cork' opposite the entrance to Charles Fort. New houses flank it at the start. When we reach the Kinsale AFC ground, on the right, not only is the lighthouse visible on the Old Head, but the ruined signal tower at the landward end. Also, James Fort, with Duggan Bridge and the Bandon mouth behind it, and the sloping fields in forty shades of green. We stay on this road for about 1.5km (1 mile). I have seen yellowhammers here, an increasingly rare bird, a merlin, once, and small charms of goldfinches.

(6) and (7) At the T-junction, we go left, and take the next left about 200m (200 yards) along, at a sign saying 'Scoil Naisiúnta' (National School). There is a brown fingerpost, with graphics of a church and a pine tree, the symbols for a Heritage Site. In this case, the graphics

St Catherine's Church of Ireland church

are remarkably accurate, for this is what we will come upon just down the road.

The road is quiet, and tree-lined. Look out for a remarkable carved capstone on a plain gate pier on the left. Next, on the right, is a fine weather-slated Georgian house, with a graceful, shallow fanlight and beautifully proportioned windows on each of the two floors. After that, it is Irish bungalows, some pretty, some plain, then a terrace of new houses and, just below it, St Catherine's Church of Ireland church, a quaint little edifice some 200 years old, set amongst trees.

(8) At the T-junction, we turn right. On the outward leg, we used the Lower Road by the water; we are taking the High Road home. Now, ahead of us all the way, we have magnificent views over harbour and town. At weekends, this road can be busy with traffic.

The views need little commentary; we see how the town fits together, terracing down from the hills to the sheltered harbour, how the great Bandon River carved its path between the rounded bulk of Castle Park and the steep escarpments on the north side above Duggan Bridge. It is a fine view, especially fine as the western sun falls on the port in the evening, and we are walking westward towards it.

(9) We now have only one last landmark to watch out for in order to make this a loop walk. On the right, 300m (328 yards) before the Spaniards corner there are fat, black-and-yellow bollards marking a tarred path descending steeply and providing a short route down to Scilly Well, our starting point. If one passes a sign on the left indicating 'Scilly Walking Tour', one has gone too far.

This steep path is the aforementioned Breakheart Hill. At Scilly Well, a path with steps climbs up the opposite slope and reaches the R600 road to Cork, which it crosses. This is known as Featherbed Lane because Kinsale girls, wooed by British soldiers serving at Charles Fort and living in the military housing just off the lane, were seduced here. Later, finding them pregnant, their feckless lovers would bid them goodbye on Breakheart Hill.

Kinsale marinas

BROWN'S MILLS WALK

Key points: Out of town via The Glen – Waterlands – Oysterhaven Creek – Brown's Mills – Clasheen Cross – return to town via Friar's Gate

Start/finish: Kinsale Post Office, grid ref.: W638504

Distance: 5–6.5km (3 to 4 miles)
Map: OSi Sheet 87 **Walking time:** I hour 30 minutes approx.

(1) At the exit from the Post Office, we turn right and go right again at the Fisherman's Market at the top of the street, a historic building, now a café-bar-restaurant. This takes us up The Glen for 90m (100 yards). Before the land between it and the sea was reclaimed, The Glen was a dock serving the inner harbour, with warehouses and bondhouses on the water. At the end of The Glen, we reach Brewery Corner, once the site of Cuckoo Mill where corn was ground and rape seed pressed for oil to keep the light of the Old Head beacon burning.

(2) Passing the old terracotta-painted Fire Station, with '*Comhairle an Bhaile Cheann tSáile*' (Kinsale Town Council) above the door, we ignore the main road sweeping left and ascend the steep hill to the right, unsigned but known locally as Trooper's Hill. We pass a 'Yield' sign, where a road enters from the right, and continue, passing St Multose Community Hall and School. We reach Henry Good's Mill, on our left.

(3) Just beyond the mill, we reach a T-junction and turn right on a wide road. Here, we may pause to look back at fine views of the inner harbour. After passing the mill on our left, we are now definitely 'in the country'.

(4) We take a narrow lane on the left, just before a large guest house, 'Waterlands'. Tarmacadam persists for a few hundred metres, with

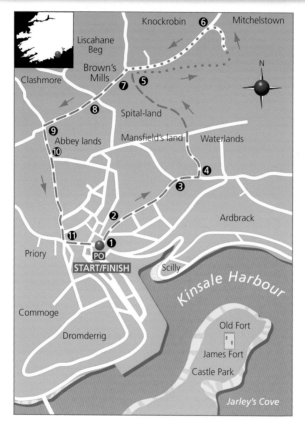

some houses. The way is gravelled, before becoming a grassy track. After 0.5km (0.35 miles), continue following the track as it curves left, ignoring a narrower track with grass at centre seen straight ahead. Descend steeply between bushes of flowering blackthorn and may-blossom in spring, with primroses and violets in profusion along the banks. Later, these are replaced by tall foxgloves and the bushes, then green, are bedecked in honeysuckle. There is a stand of tall, golden evening primrose halfway down, and a watercourse which may make the going soggy. In winter, the bushes bear haws and sloes,

Brown's Mills, restored

and redwings, fieldfares and thrushes, arriving ravenous from the Scandinavian winter, descend upon them to gorge their fill. Bullfinches are also a feature of this green road, flitting from bush to bush, easily spotted by their brilliant white rump.

There will be glimpses of the headwaters of Oysterhaven Creek below us to the right. In winter, this path may be wet in places, and one should take care.

As we descend, we get a view of the creek below on our right. We reach the small, tarred road at Brown's Mills. Here, grouped around the creek head, is an attractive hamlet of old stone houses, a country pub – the Oyster Creek Bar – overlooking the creek where wild duck dabble. Opposite the bar is a large stone building, the eponymous mill: a three-storey watermill built in 1598 and recently sympathetically renovated. A pictorial plaque in front maps the sites of the Battle of Kinsale.

(5) Beyond the Oyster Creek Bar is a brightly painted small cottage, with a stream running close by. We turn right beside it and immediately on the right is a gap that leads into a lane, an old road that is now

private property. When I included it in an earlier guide, the owner was good enough to allow walkers to pass along it and enjoy the waterside flora and fauna. Walkers using this path must be aware that it is private and they do so at their own discretion. If it is now closed or impassable, we must forego the short loop of which it is part, and retrace our steps to the mill and move to the route described in (7) below.

We take this and cross a small stone bridge. A grassy path leads right, to the creek head. Follow this. A heap of fish nets and home-made lobster pots lies beside the hedge. Just beyond is a field gate: please close it after passing. When the tide is out, a small channel on the right winds between the gravel and mud banks, with emerald green weed swirling in the slow current. Herons fish in the shallows, and redshank and curlew stalk the mud. This stream holds the fry of flatfish, and small eels, in summer. Gently lift a stone, and a fish will dart out in a flurry of sand. Glittering dragonflies and damselflies are attracted by the water.

In early summer, white lilac on the ditches greets the walker to this old roadway. It is now a quiet green lane, climbing gently, occasionally used by tractors and often muddy after wet weather.

Beyond the briary hedges, fields slope down to the shores of the creek. The laneway, on a sunny day, is idyllic, with butterflies everywhere – speckled woods, red admirals, painted ladies – and the drone of carder, bumblebees and honeybees. Cow parsley and angelica grows along the ditches – also, some hogweed, which should be avoided because it raises painful weals on the skin.

At the top of the lane, there is tin-roofed shed and a gateway on the right affording a fine view of the new bridge on the R600 and a sweep of new blacktop highway below. Both Oysterhaven Creek and the Belgooly River are visible in the wide panorama from this high place.

The next 8m (20 yards) can be very difficult in wet weather, when the path is boggy or a large pool collects. Beyond it, the path climbs, and arrives at a gate, with an old whitewashed, slated shed on the right. The gate should be carefully closed after we pass through.

A large, detached 1950s' or 1960s' house stands in a raised garden on the left. On the right, we pass what was once a classical Irish farmyard: low, whitewashed buildings on two-and-a-half sides. It is now in disuse. Ivy fills the windows and has colonised the old thatch under the tin roof, red with rust. New corrugated-iron barns now tower over it. But this yard is private property, and should not be trespassed upon. The pathway continues, and passes another long, low house gable on the right before it reaches a T-junction at a narrow, tarred road.

(6) We are on top of a hill, between Knockrobin and Mitchelstown. There are modern bungalows on the road to our right. We turn left and pass the concrete enclosure of a wayside water pump, now gone, and set off downhill. This is a lovely road, narrow, with overgrown hedges and burgeoning fecundity, a botanist's feast. Glimpses are to be had of the creek below, and the gorse banks on the other side. Hart's-tongue ferns grow to prodigious lengths in the shelter of the high ditches. On the left, we have blackthorn, whitethorn and ash; on the right, big trees – ash, beech, sycamore and field maple – shading the road. It is a sun-dappled, old fashioned road, so quiet that we often see rabbits grazing in the roadside fields, or cock pheasants strutting about the winter ploughland.

On the right, large gate piers and a sweeping entrance lead down a driveway to an elegant Georgian house with a fine fanlight and five windows on the first floor. A view of Brown's Mills, in the valley, is to be had at the gateway. Just below is a small lodge, with roses draping its impressive stone gateway. At the bottom of the slope, we pass the creek-side pathway we took earlier, and recross the bridge to come out again facing Brown's Mills.

(7) Just past the Oyster Creek Bar, an uphill road must be climbed, steep but short. At the top, at Pike Cross, we come to a main road, the R607. Before crossing it, we may pause to read the plaque on the left which tells us that this high ground was the site of the English camp in 1601, with a force of 6,600 foot and 650 horse under Mountjoy besieging the Spanish force of 4,000 in Kinsale (see Scilly and Charles Fort Walk). The English camp then straddled what was the old road to Cork. There was a turnpike, or toll gate here once, hence the name 'Pike Cross'.

(8) We enter the small road almost opposite the plaque, numbered L3214. This would have been the route taken by English forces to the battle site. It is a quiet country road, climbing slightly, with some

Oyster Creek

houses on the right. We cross the route of the old railway and, at the next cross (9), turn left onto the R605, going slightly downhill towards the town. At a Y-junction sign (10), we take the 'narrow' leg, which is straight ahead. The hospital, across a field on our left, was originally a workhouse for the destitute. Our road crosses the site of the old burial grounds. There is now a new housing estate, Abbey Fort, on the right, with a broad pavement outside. On the left, opposite where the pavement ends, there is a gate and a turnstile. On one of the gateposts, a limestone plaque commemorates the site as 'An Poll Buí, The Great Famine 1845–1995'. The date is, of course, confusing but the name *An Poll Buí* means 'The Yellow Hole', so called because of the many starving and cholera-stricken bodies that were interred there. A memorial cross stands in an area of mown grass, entered via a gate and stile.

At the top of the hill, we have our first glimpses of Kinsale, below us. We enter the town via the Friary Gate, an ancient town gate through which Carmelite friars walked from their abbey lands, close by. Father Matthew, 'The Apostle of Temperance', passed triumphantly through this gate, led by bands and sober crowds, in 1844.

(11) The descending road curves gently left towards the town centre with St Multose Church straight ahead. In front of it, we go left, and this brings us into the Market Square. Rounding the Market House, with the ancient anchor against the wall, we emerge in Pearse Street, opposite The Fisherman's Market and The Blue Haven. Our starting point, the Post Office, is just down the street.

TIMOLEAGUE AND ARGIDEEN RIVER WALK

> **Key points:** Historic abbey, castle, chapel and courthouse – Argideen river valley – wooded by-roads – wild flowers – views over village and bay

Start/finish: the car park behind Timoleague Abbey, grid ref.: W472438

Map: OSi Sheet 86 or 89
Distance: 7.2km (4.3 miles) **Walking Time:** 2 to 3 hours

(1) We begin at the car park behind Timoleague Abbey, where a gate enters the ruins. The village name is an anglicisation of *Tig Molaga*, meaning 'the House of Molaga', having been established on the site of a seventh-century monastery founded by Saint Molaga, a holy man who devoted himself to the care of plague victims and died on 20 January AD 665 of the plague.

Two booklets detailing the abbey's long history are available in the local shops, so I will simply skim the story.

The Annals of the Four Masters tell us that the foundations of the present abbey were laid by a McCarthy chieftain in 1240, the site having been a place of pilgrimage since Molaga's time. The local Norman family, the De Barras (Barrys), had a greater or lesser input. In 1400, the enclave was given to the Franciscan Order. Already it had become customary for the dead of local noble families to be buried within the grounds. So many were buried there that, after four centuries, remains were disinterred and built into an ossuary wall of skulls and bones to make room for new burials. The poem at the gate, by an eighteenth-century poet, records this. Respect for the dead of local families buried around and within the abbey has been an impediment to its restoration.

Timoleague Abbey was famous for its library, and was visited by the writers of the Annals of the Four Masters. There may have been a Book of Timoleague to rival The Book of Kells. The village was a

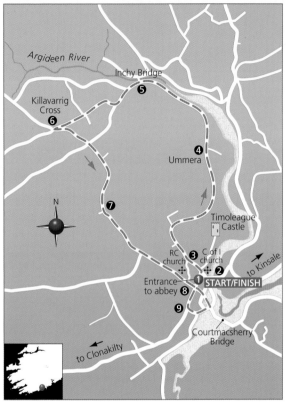

Argideen River

Inchy Bridge

5

Killavarrig
Cross
6

4
Ummera

N

7

Timoleague
Castle

RC **3** C of I
church church

to Kinsale

Entrance **2**
to abbey **8** **1** START/FINISH

9

Courtmacsherry
Bridge

to Clonakilty

centre of commerce before Bandon town was even founded, and the friars are known to have conducted a thriving trade in wine.

(2) Exiting the abbey via the same gate, we turn left and walk down a wide pedestrian path along the graveyard wall. After crossing the road to the near side of the Courtmacsherry bridge, we make our way left along the grass verge beside the water. Passing the picnic tables, we shortly meet the main road at the bridge spanning the River Argideen. It is worth crossing the road to lean on the parapet and look up-river for a classic view of Timoleague House and castle. Egrets, small white

Timoleague Abbey and village

storks new to Ireland, favour the riverside trees, often reflected in the placid brown waters. The castle, in ruins, stands behind the house. It was built by the de Barrys in 1214, shortly after the Norman invasion of Ireland – in fact, the Barrys arrived in Ireland before Strongbow. Over the centuries, it changed hands between Barrys and McCarthys, Norman and Irish overlords, often in violent circumstances. A pamphlet, authored by Robert Travers, present owner of the house and lands, provides the vivid details.

During the 'Troubles' of the 1920s, the castle was garrisoned, and badly damaged by an explosion. It was later partly demolished when it endangered the nearby railway line – the Timoleague and Courtmacsherry Light Railway – which ran along the Argideen banks beneath its walls. The house was burnt by the IRA in the early 1920s, but was rebuilt in 1923 using the same stones.

(3) Facing upriver, we turn left and follow the church wall, which rounds a corner to the right. The Church of Ireland chapel, within the walls, is unique. The grounds are lovely, with mature yews and a small, well-kept graveyard. But it is the interior which brings the surprise. Tiled in exotic mosaic, the south wall resembles more a corner of the Taj Mahal than an Irish country chapel interior.

Leaving the church, we turn right and immediately arrive at the gates of Timoleague House and gardens.

Our route passes the gates, and sets off out of the village, passing the imposing Catholic church on the left. This, built on a site given by the Travers family, was completed in 1912, and has a fine window on the west side, added in 1931, the work of an Irish master of stained glass, Harry Clarke. The ancient Timoleague Chalice, with which the last abbey friars fled during Penal times, was found in a house on Cape Clear Island in 1856, and is now once again in the keeping of the parish.

The large house on the left is the Glebe House, which was the Church of Ireland vicar's residence. On the right, the high stone walls of Timoleague House estate follow the road. Old stone walls in southwest Ireland are vertical gardens, supporting a wide and fecund growth of plants. Here, as elsewhere, we will find navelwort with bell-like flowers shooting to 50cm (20 inches) tall, wall rue and delicate maidenhair, herb Robert, with pink flowers, bright purple violets, white stitchworth, and even foxgloves, which may be 2m (6.5ft) tall, sometimes gain a hold.

Meanwhile, depending on the time of year, the verges may be blue with bluebells, white with ransoms, creamy with primroses or

Timoleague House on the River Argideen

golden with buttercups. Stands of beeches line the estate walls, and then a stand of conifers. Below, the Argideen estuary can be glimpsed and Courtmacsherry Bay with, above it, the heights of Barreragh (see next walk).

(4) We are walking on the high land over the western bank of the Argideen. Warblers may be heard in spring and summer, along with long-eared owls and the raucous cackling of pheasants. In winter, foraging bands of long tailed tits are a regular feature, and goldcrests can be seen in the pines. A sparrowhawk occupies an old pigeon nest near the gateway to Ummera House.

Ummera House nowadays produces exclusive smoked wild salmon. The house is set in fine pastures, with a tree-lined drive typical of the 'planter's house' of the eighteenth century. It commands views of the river, and fishing rights along its frontage. The road-facing wall below a modern cottage on the left is an excellent example of Irish stone-wall construction, with the stones set vertically, rather than horizontally.

Beyond Ummera, a small tributary crosses beneath the road, lined with alder and salix (sally trees).

Argideen Vale Lawn Tennis and Croquet Club

Sea trout and salmon pool below Inchy Bridge

The grass courts and pavilion of the Argideen Vale Lawn Tennis and Croquet Club are on the left. We pass an unedifying chicken-fattening unit on the right. Soon, marsh marigolds and flag irises carpet the wet ground by the river below us. After tunnels of trees edged with thick leaf mould where wood anemones grow in spring and tasty wood blewitts and parasol mushrooms in winter, we come to Inchy Bridge.

The Argideen has long been one of Munster's most famous sea trout and salmonid rivers. Here, volunteer labour and a LEADER grant have created wheelchair access to allow the disabled to fish immediately in front of the picturesque bridge. Over this pool, in summer, bats flit, including Daubenton's, the water bat. Kingfishers are resident, and dippers, the small birds that walk beneath the water and hunts between the riverbed stones.

(5) We do not cross the bridge, but continue straight ahead to the Barryroe Co-op building and a signpost for Ballinascarthy and Clonakilty. We see, 100m (330 yards) ahead, fishing lodges sensitively restored from ancient stone barns by Tim Severin, explorer and author of *The Brendan Voyage*. However, we bear left, past a house with many-headed cordyline palms. Shortly, a road goes off to our left; we can take this and shorten our walk by perhaps 1km (0.6 miles).

But, continuing to the right, we pass another house with hydra-headed palms and a plain, straight country road to Killavarrig Cross Roads.

(6) Here, we turn left, doubling back up the hill. The climb is steep but short, and as we ascend we get wonderful panoramic views of the country to the west and north of us, large, rich fields, scrubby woodlands, and hilltops with heather and gorse. We pass through a crossroads – the road plunging down to the left is the access from the shorter route, mentioned earlier. Now, on these high lands, we can see for miles. Wild strawberries are common on the roadside ditches.

At a brake of gorse, and a gurgling stream, a dog-leg turn takes us up another short steep climb. 'No fox hunting', requests a notice on a gate.

(7) On this road, there are three climbs between Killavarrig and the 'summit' at Ardmore, but there are breaks between them, and none is very long or steep. At Ardmore, there is a farm with extensive outbuildings, and then we set off downhill towards Timoleague. The road is straight and, immediately, we have a magnificent view of Courtmacsherry Bay, Courtmacsherry itself to the east, with Wood Point beyond, and Harbour View opposite.

Steeply descending, we pass bungalows, and verges where orange montbretia, a garden escape now wild in Ireland, grows in profusion, and lords-and-ladies, those unusual lily-like plants.

First, we see the spire of the Catholic church, then a gable of the Abbey, then the Argideen, and Timoleague House and the Castle. The Abbey layout is clearly seen from here, the tower rising at the centre, the chapels and library, the graveyard to one side. The painted houses of Timoleague appear, shocking pink, papal purple, tropical azure and apple green: the Irish are, indeed, fearless with paint! A copse of trees beyond the bridge across the bay is a flourishing rookery.

(8) Reaching the centre of the village, at the crossroads we turn right. On the left is an imposing building, with five arches. Built in about 1696, it initially served as a market house on the ground floor, and an Assizes Court above. Bought and restored from semi-dereliction by this writer and his wife, it is now a school where students come from all over the globe to learn the English language. In 1821, riots by the Catholic Irish

against demands to pay tithes to Protestant clergy led to a murder for which local men were to be arraigned. Daniel O'Connell, 'The Liberator', arrived unexpectedly to defend them, whether successfully or not is not known. A brass plaque commemorates his visit.

(9) At the corner, we turn left and pass the filling station. If it is evening and low tide, and any time between October and April, the slob in front of the metal bridge is likely to be carpeted in birds. Huge flocks of lapwing and golden plover rise and fly in intricate formations again and again before settling down. Redshank and curlew wing in to roost, and tiny dunlin flash and turn in dazzling display. Ducks and swans drift quietly in the shallow pools.

Walking along the water, with the playing field on the left, we reach the north end of the bridge. Opposite, a closed walkway leads, through bollards, to the Abbey entrance, and we are back where we began.

Courtmacsherry Bay and Courtmacsherry from above Timoleague

BARRERAGH AND ABBEYMAHON WALK

Key points: west end of Courtmacsherry village – Siberia – woods of Earl of Shannon estate – elevated views of Courtmacsherry Bay with Timoleague and abbey – Abbeymahon Monastery ruins – wading bird roost

Start/finish: the pier in Courtmacsherry, grid ref.: W508427

Distance: 7.5km (4.5 miles)
Map: OSi Sheet 87 **Walking Time:** 2 hours

Courtmacsherry is a linear village, population 200 in winter, with brightly painted houses lining the single pavement, and the bay on the opposite side of the road. It is sheltered by old woods, behind.

The name derives from *Cúirt Mhic Shéafraidh*, the court of the son of Geoffrey, Geoffrey being a name adopted by the Norman Hodnett family when they 'became more Irish than the Irish themselves'. The village has long been a small resort, and many Cork business families have had holiday homes here for generations.

(1) We begin our walk at the pier. Sea angling boats operate from here all summer, taking anglers out to fish the numerous local ship-wrecks or to catch sharks, which are tagged and returned to the sea. A few small fishing boats also operate.

The most impressive craft to be seen in the channel today is the Courtmacsherry lifeboat. It is notable that, from the small population, the hamlet provides enough brave volunteers to man the lifeboat whatever the weather.

Above the village may be seen the old Coast Guard Station. The largest fortified Coast Guard Station in Ireland – the gun ports may still be seen – it was built about 1869 and torched by the rebel Irish in 1922 when, it was said, 'the Irish burnt everything British except their coal'. The building was extensively renovated in 1972 and converted to holiday apartments.

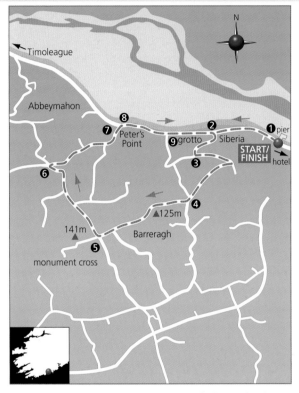

Leaving the pier, we pass the wooden Railway Station, now a private dwelling. The railway was closed in 1961.

As we walk, we see Burren Pier across the bay, here only 1km (0.6 miles) wide. The grassy right-hand verge follows the track of the old railway along the bay to Timoleague. A large painted map by the roadside illustrates the Seven Heads and the coast from Wood Point to Dunworly. On it, we can trace the route we will be taking, south to the uplands, and circling back down to Abbeymahon and the sea. The overlordship of the Norman De Barras (Barrys) is evident in the place names – Barryroe, Barry's Point, Travara, etc. Also illustrated are the positions of shipwrecks, including the *Lusitania*, and the positions of signal towers along the coast. There is a pleasant picnic table in front of the map, and one of the large anchors of the *Cardiff Hall*, sunk with all hands off the Seven Heads in 1925 (see Seven Heads Walk) is displayed close by.

The Community Hall is on the right, and, on the left, a grotto of the Virgin Mary, followed by a terrace of brightly painted council houses. This end of Courtmacsherry is called, even on the maps, 'Siberia', although the presence of palms in the park and gardens surely refutes this dire slur and evidences Courtmacsherry's rightful Riviera reputation!

(2) We turn sharp left just before the Grotto. A green path can be seen leading to the woods above. On summer evenings, an amazing number of pipistrelle bats issues from the eaves at the back of one of the nearby modern houses, a veritable river of bats flowing into the darkening air.

The green pathway winds to the right, making the climb more gentle, and ascends between ivied stone walls to the woodland above. We begin to get elevated views of the bay. These woods are part of the old Earl of Shannon estate, recorded as sheltering the village from 'the sea-winds' in Smith's *History of Cork* (1750). The Earl of Shannon acquired the lands about that time, and planted further woods at the harbour mouth. There are many exotics, including an ancient cork oak in front of the hotel, the earl's one-time summer residence. These woods lend Courtmacsherry its classic 'chocolate-box' beauty, mirror-still water reflecting multicoloured boats and houses, and stately woods behind.

Blacktailed godwit, certain to be seen on a bayshore walk in winter

Thousands of gulls, Courtmacsherry Bay

The track climbs the wooded slope. As we reach the last trees, we turn right off the main track (which continues to a tarred road after 200m/220 yards) and follow a narrow woodland path. The path runs due west, winding through the trees. Below, the backs of the village houses, and glimpses of the bay, limited or extensive depending on the foliage and the time of year.

(3) The path ends at steps set into a stone wall, and we walk 20m (22 yards) along a raised ditch to join a narrow, gently ascending tarred road, with two new houses opposite. Looking back, we can enjoy the first of many fine views of the bay.

We turn left, climbing gradually. In winter, flocks of gulls, curlews and black-and-white oystercatchers forage on the fields on either side. We are briefly walking east now. Ahead, we see the wide strip of woodland that backs the village and runs down the western arm of the bay to Wood Point. Tucked in to the right are the new houses of Meadowlands estate, almost screened by trees in summer. Across the bay mouth beyond, we see Coolmain Strand and Coolmain Castle, owned by the Walt Disney family. Directly opposite us, across the estuary, is the Burren House, a fine Georgian residence amidst trees. There are many such 'planter's houses' between here and Bandon, 14.5km (9 miles) away.

As we turn a sharp corner and head west again, we see another such house across the bay, Lisheen, one of the old houses of the Scott family, who still own much of the land around it. The slope continues, pleasantly energetic. The roadside vegetation is hart's-tongue, hard fern and navelwort, with occasional blackthorns and fuchsias. We pass a house called '*Suaimhneas*' (peace), with a new dwelling just beyond, and arrive at a staggered crossroads. The first right turn plunges steeply back towards the bay.

(4) We take the second right (more or less straight ahead – see map), still climbing gently. We are soon at Barreragh or *Barr Aerach* ('Airy Top'), a bracing spot with the best views for miles. Roadside gorse and whitethorn bloom in season. Far below and to the left is the inner bay, with the many coloured houses of Timoleague village climbing the hill, and the ruins of thirteenth-century Timoleague Abbey by the water. Gleaming wetlands, where flocks of wading birds roost, lie beside the estuary of the River Argideen. Beyond Timoleague, the hills of West Cork stretch to the horizon.

Turning 180°, we see, 9.5km (6 miles) off, the wide mouth of the bay, mile-long Garretstown Strand, the long arm of the Old Head of Kinsale, its lighthouse, and the open Atlantic. To the southeast, across the peninsula, Barry's Point is visible, and it is possible to make out the old Lifeboat Station, halfway along the headland, from whence a lifeboat that reached the *Lusitania* was launched.

Courtmacsherry Bay from Barreragh

IRA memorial, Barreragh

(5) At the next crossroads, an iron cross stands on a plinth painted green, white and gold, surrounded by a wrought-iron railing, slightly out of true. This is a memorial cross for an IRA volunteer who died in a skirmish with British forces during the War of Independence. It is a lonely place, where a single gnarled tree stands behind the cross, and the four winds blow.

We turn right now, and start downhill towards the bay. Below us, the ruined gable of the old church of Abbeymahon can be seen between the trees. The boreen is sheltered by high ditches, and the student of botany will enjoy the wealth of wild plants growing amongst the gorse and the ferns. The sorrel is particularly good to eat, sharp and sour on the palate.

(6) After the road levels, we come to a four-cross roads* (see alternative route below) where we turn right, staying on this road until we reach the shore at Ballynamona Cross, and go left 180m (200 yards) to visit the ruins at Abbeymahon (7).

As an alternative, we may continue straight ahead at the cross and continue along an unsurfaced lane, adding 1.5km (1 mile) to the walk. In winter, the first section, running between farmyards, is extremely muddy, but a right turn at the next T-junction takes us quickly along a paved boreen to a pleasant 'green road' beneath beeches and thence downhill to the bay shore. In this case, we turn right and immediately come upon the ruins at Abbeymahon.

Sometime before 1272, Cistercian monks moved from their first house at Aghmanister, near Timoleague, to Abbeymahon where they remained until the monastery was suppressed in 1537. The surviving gable of an ancient keep attached to the monastery stands on private land nearby.

Turning to walk the 1km (0.6 miles) back to Courtmacsherry, we immediately pass a stand of low reeds just offshore. Between October and March, four varieties of duck may be seen feeding here. Most obvious are the large, elegant shelduck. Present here, also, are tiny teal, with swept-back Chinese eyes and plumage that gleams like lacquer when it catches the light. Widgeon, with ruddy heads and white wing bars, and glossy-headed mallard also feed amongst the reeds.

(8) About 45m (50 yards) after Ballynamona Cross, we pass Peter's Point, a small, low promontory inside the sea wall. This seemingly insignificant outcrop is of immense importance as a high-tide roost for waders and literally hundreds of tiny dunlin, ringed plover, godwits, redshank, greenshank, lapwing, whimbrel, and curlew crowd together

Abbeymahon graveyard with Courtmacsherry Bay   Abbeymahon with primroses

on the margins when the tide is high. We pass quietly; the birds ignore cars but are easily disturbed by walkers. Hereabouts, a peregrine falcon is regularly seen raising the flocks, or perched on the roadside fence posts after feeding.

Back, then, along the bayside path to the village, a laudable initiative created in 2001 and much used by visitors and locals alike. Running from Timoleague to Courtmacsherry, the 5km (3-mile) long paved pathway makes wonderful use of the grassy verge between road and sea upon which the Timoleague and Courtmacsherry Extension Light Railway once ran. Near Timoleague, wayside plaques depict the various bird species in full colour, with attendant information, these made by Peter Wolstenholme, the Courtmacsherry potter, expert bird-watcher, skilled artist and master ceramicist.

(9) It is a lovely walk along the bay and only a short distance before we reach *Cois Cuan* and Harbour Court, both new estates.

Now a series of displays and artefacts greet the walkers at the edge of the village. First, there is a pretty sign with the village name in English and Irish and a cameo picture of the Courtmacsherry Lifeboat, of which the village is rightly proud. Nearby, is a limestone plaque inscribed with the logo and the history of the railway and a second nameplate, modelled on that of the old station and mounted on ancient wooden piles, once the submerged supports of the old pier. Now, after the car park, on the right we see the Catholic church and a row of brightly painted houses facing the children's playground, where cordyline palm trees grow. We next pass the Community Hall, once the village school, after which, on a green lawn, are some picnic tables, with maps and sketches of the estuary birds adjacent, mounted on boards, and one of the two anchors from the *Cardiff Hall* steamship, which sank off Travara Cove in 1925 (see Seven Heads to Travara Cove Walk). We soon reach the pier, the end of our itinerary.

Courtmacsherry is a very pretty village and, if we continue, we will pass a row of fine, Georgian houses, Hamilton Terrace, some detached, some terraced, facing the bay. At the eastern end of the village is the Courtmacsherry Hotel, once the summer residence of the Earl of Shannon. It has one of Ireland's two only cork trees on its front lawn, a magnificent old specimen never stripped for its cork. Opposite and beyond the hotel is the beach, then woodland walks and pleasant coves.

SEVEN HEADS TO TRAVARA COVE WALK

Key points: Shanagh, a partly restored 'famine' village — Travara Cove — cliffs and wild coastal scenery

Start/finish: Narry's Cross on the Timoleague coast road from Butlerstown, grid ref.: W504389

Distance: 7.5km (4.5 miles)
Map: OSi Sheet 87 **Walking Time:** 2 to 3 hours

---

(1) Park the car at Narry's Cross. The simplest way to find Narry's Cross is to drive through Butlerstown from the west (houses and shops on the left), pass the Community Hall (on the left) and continue for 800m (0.5 miles) to the brown signpost saying 'Timoleague. Coast Road. 10km'. This is Narry's Cross. There is a triangle of grass between the roads where one may park.

From Narry's Cross we can see the route, straight ahead, downhill towards the open Atlantic, which is roughly 3.2km (2 miles) distant. Pause to enjoy the 180° view of the broad, green landscape dotted with scattered farms and a few trees. To the right (the west) lies the Galley Head, with its lighthouse, the westerly arm of Clonakilty Bay. Set off down the road towards the sea.

A lone cottage on the right, with a few wind-torn trees for shelter. Continue straight across the four-cross-roads.

This was once Poor Law land, and the old, simple farmhouses still standing, the ruins and stone-walled fields attest the bitter struggle for mere subsistence. But times have changed. Since the foundation of the state, Barryroe has been known for its 'strong farmers'. The land is good and there are many large farmhouses with well-kept yards and barns. Where houses fell into ruins, there have been strangers to buy and renovate them. The wild coast that reminds the native of famine and emigration seems to the misanthropic city dweller a haven from stress, traffic, people, a landscape where spirit-nurturing Nature still rules supreme.

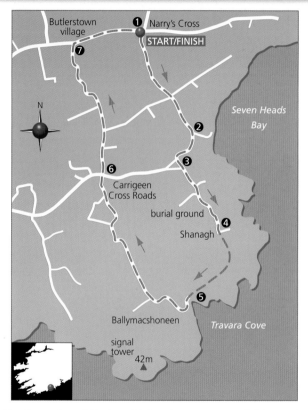

Continue downhill. An old farmhouse across fields to the left, with a wind-torn macrocarpa pine in front. This is windy country, with the 'sceac' bushes (blackthorns) growing out of the low stone walls, sculpted into tortured shapes by the southwesterlies sweeping in from the coast in winter storms. Hart's-tongue ferns on the stone walls along the lane are salt burnt, even though nearly 1km (0.6 miles) from the sea.

(2) There is a Y in the road, where a stream passes under via a culvert. The left leg of the Y plunges down to Coosnaluinga Cove, while the

right leg continues our route and climbs steeply towards the sky. Divert to the cove for a few minutes; it is worthwhile. The lane follows the stream, gushing down a deep, ferny ravine, and descends steeply to a small, pebble beach, with a short slipway and a concrete path leading across sea-rock outcrops to a platform, suitable for docking boats or for swimmers to dive off in summer.

It is a lonely place, rarely visited. Acorn barnacles, seed mussels, limpets, periwinkles, whelks and sea anemones are everywhere on the rocks. From March to October, the rock pools are full of life, miniature, perfect aquariums, resplendent with red coralline, green sea lettuce, yellow carrageen moss. Small, highly specialised fish like shannies, blennies and rockling hide in the clear depths, along with many species of prawns, crabs, starfish and brittle stars.

The lone house above the cove must enjoy one of the finest views in Ireland, looking out across Courtmacsherry Bay to the distant beaches of Garretstown and the cliffs of the Old Head of Kinsale. From the laneway approaching it, one may share this view.

Returning to the main route, one now climbs a few hundred metres of steep road, passing a neat, well-kept farmhouse. Far behind us is Courtmacsherry Bay; ahead Clonakilty Bay and the Galley Head. At the top of the hill, we take the track that follows the wall around to the left, past a field gate. This high point commands 360° views. About 3.2km (2 miles) to the north, across wide, rich fields, is the village of Butlerstown, its single street of multicoloured houses facing us. To the south is the wide Atlantic; to the east, Courtmacsherry Bay, bounded by the distant cliffs of the Old Head; to the west, in the middle distance, the coves of Dunworly, white surf breaking on dark rocks, with small sandy beaches in between.

(3) We continue, following the wall on the left side of the track, and join the paved road again after 25m (30 yards). Our route now leads straight for the sea. Ignore the road on the right, going west to Carrigeen Cross Roads. On each side, Connemara-style stone walls, patterned with white lichen, divide sizeable, rolling fields. To the right is a track marked on the OS map, leading to old burial grounds. It passes through a farmyard and is much used by cattle. In wet weather it cannot be negotiated with less than rubber boots.

(4) At the end of the paved road, we reach Shanagh, once a grey village of eleven or so stone houses that never knew plaster or paint and had, since the Famine period, fallen into ruin. Some are large; all but one were abandoned until the sudden surge in renovating old properties during the Celtic Tiger years. It is an ancient settlement, its name deriving from *seantoir*, the Irish for sanctuarium, referring to a church or burial ground, the memory of which has been preserved in the name for some 1,300 years. The burial ground is close by.

Find the track leaving the village between the ruins to the right. There is a track to the left but it is a quagmire, and comes to a dead end in a field. The track we follow is a surviving section of a 'famine road', leading from the nearby hamlet of Ballinluig to Coostravarra (Travara Cove), a 'public works' project set up in 1847 to provide famine relief in return for work. This old road may be extremely muddy in winter.

This famine road leads through stone-walled fields towards the sea. Off to the right, we see a signal tower erected in 1804–06, and two observation posts looking out to sea. This tower is within view of towers to the east, at the Old Head, and to the west, at Galley Head.

The track leading up from Travara Cove

The Old Head of Kinsale, from Poulna Point

The idea was to ring the south coast with a communications system for fear the French would again invade, as they had in 1796 and 1798.

(5) History records that, in the 1840s, a pier was built at Travara Cove, also as part of the Famine Relief Programme. Only a short boat slip is to be seen today. It is hard to believe that a pier would last long in the massive seas that wash into Travara in winter.

On 13 January 1925, a large vessel, the *Cardiff Hall*, on the last lap of its voyage from Argentina to Cork with a cargo of maize, ran aground on the vicious Shoonta Rock off Travara Cove, with the loss of all twenty-seven souls aboard. The lifeboat, now stationed at Courtmacsherry but then at Barry's Point, was launched; however, the ferocity of the gale made it impossible to row around the point to bring assistance. One of the anchors of the *Cardiff Hall* is displayed beside the main (and only) street in Butlerstown, the other on the grass verge at the western end of Courtmacsherry.

A small stream issues onto the pebble beach at Travara, but the track (clearly marked on the OS map) that once followed its eastern bank and met the paved road east of Carrigeen Cross Roads is now impassable. Instead, we cross the stream and take the road that climbs from the boat slip. An old winch stands in the hedge on the right, rusted and decaying. On the other side of the stream, a few stones upon stones mark the ruins of an ancient cottage. The village of Butlerstown, 3.2km (2 miles) off, is framed in the 'V' of the craggy, gorse-grown ravine down which the stream runs.

We are now in the townland and hamlet of Ballymacshoneen. The name 'Shoneen' is derogatory in some parts of Ireland. It may come from 'Seánín', meaning 'little Seán', and has no pejorative echoes here.

We pass an old roadside pump, once the only local water supply. Until recently, it has continued to deliver sweet water, faintly flavoured with iron oxide, a not unpleasant tang. It was tested nitrate-free some years ago, although nitrate traces, from fertiliser run-off, showed in most local groundwater at that time. If it still functions, drink at your own risk. Butlerstown is straight ahead, a line of colourful houses facing us about 3km (2 miles) away, and refreshment galore is available there. As we walk towards it, the field walls are a cornucopia of lichens, hard fern, hart's-tongue, navelwort and small, flowering succulents.

This is a land of ancient ring forts, with seven identified between Shanagh and Dunworly alone. In a field to the left of the road is a well-preserved example, about 30m (100ft) in diameter, with encircling ramparts rising about 1.5m (4 or 5ft) above the sward. These forts proliferated on the landscape in the early Christian period, the fifth to the tenth century. The perimeter banks marked farmyards, not fortresses, the wooden structures inside having long since decayed. The earthworks are brown with dead ferns and gorse in winter, bright green and orange in summer, with the whiff of coconut rising from the gorse. The country belief that these were fairy forts or 'pookeen raths' protected them from the plough.

(6) Approaching Carrigeen Cross Roads, views to the left reveal Dunworly coves and bay. We cross Carrigeen Cross Roads diametrically; the route is now quite clear, the road visible ahead. 'Carrigeen' means 'Little Rock', nothing to do with the Arkansas town or with carrageen moss, the seaweed harvested from time immemorial by the Irish, one of the few sea vegetables exploited by our conservative race.

(7) At the village 'street', we turn immediately right, and pass the Community Hall before walking the last 1km (0.6 miles) on the high road back to Narry's Cross and the car. This is a fine road for views, with a rich, green sward of grasslands stretching to the broad Atlantic and solid farmhouses dotting the land.

INCHYDONEY ISLAND

Start/finish: western end of Beamish's Lagoon, about 3.2km (2 miles) south of Clonakilty, grid ref.: W396394

Map: OSi Sheet 89
Distance: 6.5km (4 miles) **Walking Time:** 2 to 3 hours.

This loop walk is best taken on a low or falling tide.

(1) We set out from the western end of Beamish's Lagoon, a favourite venue for 'twitching' birders because it sometimes holds exotic birds.

Beamish's Lagoon is a local name; no name appears on the OS map. It is reached by driving along the western side of Clonakilty Bay, past Youghals. Do not take any of the right turnings; the sea is kept constantly on the left. A sign is reached which says 'Cul de sac'. Continue, with the water on the left until one arrives at a right turning at the western end of a small lake, separated from the sea by the road. Begin the walk here.

We set off, taking the road inland alongside a pretty house with lattice and creeper on the walls. The marsh at the lake edge is on our left; here, it is colonised with tall Greater Reedmace or 'bullrushes', as they are commonly called. Beyond and around the reedmace is a meadow of Tussock Sedge, tall, cane-like grasses, with feathery tops, growing out of the hillocks or tussocks for which it is named.

If one moves quietly, one may see a kingfisher in the osiers along the lake margin; they are resident here. The trunks of the sallies are nicely patterned with grey-green lichen. Sallies were used for basket and lobster pot making, and for making bird traps. Alder also grows here, another typical waterside tree, colonising stream banks when its waterborne catkins take root. The catkins are soft at first but mature into small brown cones. In winter, they are a staple in the diet of siskins,

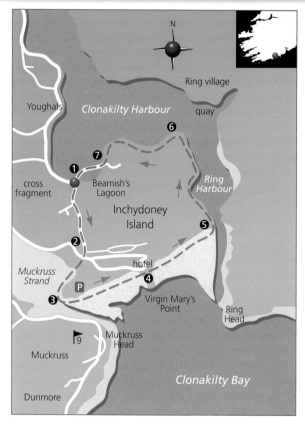

acrobatic little finches that often feed hanging upside down.

As we continue, on our left is an old perimeter wall of Inchydoney House, in places 3.5m (12ft) tall. Inchydoney Island is said to have once been the property of Elizabeth I, the previous owners having left no heirs. The Hungerford family bought it from her. Notorious landlords, they set man-traps to impale any Irish who trespassed on their grounds. Through a gap can be seen further massive walls, once enclosing an orchard or kitchen garden. As we pass, we will see the gable of an old cottage built into the perimeter wall, now ivy covered and romantic.

After a small stone cottage on the right, the road begins to ascend. The verge is host to huge, verdant ferns. From the higher ground, we now see, on the left, the house within the high walls, big and solid, with an almost Norman look. Nowadays, it is a retreat and holiday home for nuns and priests. A lane goes to the left, behind it, but we continue straight uphill on a well-worn path beside a field, climbing gently to the 'saddle' of Inchydoney Island. This path, crossing the island, has been used for millennia.

There is a ruined twelfth-century church in a field on the right, amongst a clump of trees. It was appropriated during the Reformation and the Hungerford graves are here. Away to the left, there is a monument to a 1210 battle in which the McCarthys routed the Norman De Courcys in a major defeat. There is also a collapsed souterrain and shell midden nearby, testament to the island's early settlement.

The highest point is not very high but gives the heady feeling of being on top of the world. In front is the broad Atlantic; over the centuries, a ghost ship, a demasted oak boat called the *Dearach Maol,* is said to have been seen offshore in times of tragedy. The view behind us, to the north, is panoramic, encompassing the lake, Clonakilty inner harbour, the town, and the high ground across the bay. The path goes slightly left, but we continue straight ahead, to a stile, which we pass through and thus arrive on the south slope of Inchydoney Island.

We walk downhill, through brakes of gorse on sandy soil. I once found two lizards here, as a small boy. It is quite likely there is a colony nearby: the habitat is perfect for viviparous lizards.

(2) The track reaches a point above the road but instead of descending to it, we swing left on the worn, grass path and ascend a gentle rise, parallel to the channel. From here, we have a view of the expanse of Muckruss Strand, with sandbars exposed at low tide, much frequented by wading birds. Passing behind some wooden chalets, we now descend to the road and, crossing it, continue straight down via one of the well-worn paths to the tongue of sandy beach which rounds the corner of the promontory. The sand is very fine and clean, with dashes of pebbles. On the October day when I recorded this walk, flocks of dunlin, 200 strong, skittered about the channel edge like clockwork mice or took flight in dense, acrobatic formations. They are animated and companionable birds, unlike the solitary, dignified greenshank which stalk the shallows.

(3) We round the promontory and come out onto the wide expanse of western Inchydoney Beach, a favourite with holidaymakers. Sulky races and point-to-points are sometimes held here on summer Sundays. The beach is wide, safe for swimming and a popular surfers' venue. It is also popular with a pair of otters, sometimes seen cavorting in the surf on spring evenings. Wave-rounded stones, beautifully scribbled with calcified worm tracks or acorn barnacles, are a feature on the sand. The shells of tallins, smooth cockles, rough cockles and barnacles litter the tidelines, also, sometimes, the 'Virgin Mary' shells, fragile globes, hollow, whitish, and showing a tracery of 'letters' construed, by devout persons, to read VM, or BVM. Perhaps named for the shells, the short headland of rock that divides west from east Inchydoney beach is called St Mary's Point. At low tide, there are some fine rock pools, in spring and summer alive with shannies, gobies, butterfish, pipe fish, crabs, brittle stars and sea urchins.

At the landward end of the point, the bulk of the new Inchydoney Hotel rises three storeys, somewhat dwarfing the east beach, and seen from coastline and sea for miles around. It is upmarket and luxurious. Thalassotherapy, a medical treatment based on salt water and seaweed baths, is available, one way of enjoying a soak in the briny on a winter's day.

(4) At the eastern end of the beach, steep steps ascend to the road; however, at low tide, we can go straight ahead, up the ramp and steps which climb to the car park in front of the hotel. Rock samphire grows within reach of the steps. Sea pinks, with distinctive tussocks and hold-fasts that can grip the smallest crevice in the rocks, are abundant.

Our route continues across the promontory to the beach on the other side, reached via a boat slip, via steps or, if one isn't careful, via the seat of one's pants.

Reaching the sand, we head east. A typical storm beach, there is very little jetsam, just traces of seaweed. Rough ground slopes down to it and, in spring, these wear a golden skirt of gorse, as do the slopes opposite, falling to the water before Ring Head, at the southeast tip of the channel.

We are walking towards the channel. If the tide is low, we walk comfortably along scoured sands; if it is a little higher, we may take to the rocks above the beach; if it is near full, we can proceed only by climbing the steep slopes to the fields above, but this may involve trespass on private property and is not recommended.

Inchydoney, west beach

Cinnabar moth caterpillars feeding on ragwort

(5) As the beach rounds the corner along the channel, there are quite high dunes. These are crossed by well-worn paths. By climbing the rock outcrop at the corner, a good view is gained of the village of Ring, across the channel, with Darrara Agricultural College on the high land behind, and, to the left, Clonakilty Harbour and its shores. The ground is pocked with rabbit burrows and rabbit 'currants' are everywhere. Here, also on an October walk, I found hundreds of tiny banded snails and a small crop of *hygrocybe* mushrooms with blood-red caps, orange gills and scarlet stems. They were probably *H. punicea* or *miniata*, which the books say are edible, but please don't take my word. They may be safely feasted on with the eyes, the small caps brilliant as precious stones amongst the emerald moss.

The most obvious fauna, in late summer, are the caterpillars swarming over the ragwort in Kilkenny team colours. As children, we would collect these black-and-amber crawlers – the caterpillars of the day-flying Cinnabar moth – in jam jars wherein they, sadly, shortly expired. The moths' red and black coloration deters predators; another dune species, the Six Spot Burnet moth has similar colours for defence.

Walking along the channel side, we see that there is much erosion of this sandy coast. Truncated rabbit burrows gape from the sandy banks, and the long black roots of ferns hang exposed.

After the sand gives out, the shoreline can be slippery with channelled wrack and toothed wrack in places, but when the tide is low one can comfortably walk along the pebbled shore. The toothed wrack is an estuary version, not *Fucus serratus* but *F. ceranoides*. Bladderwracks are adapted to the come and go of tides, the inbuilt bubbles, which children love to pop, being buoyancy chambers to float the weeds to the surface for light and photosynthesis. In winter, the tips have flattened, fruiting bodies.

(6) Ring village and pier, and old Ring House are now just across the channel, very close. There are large wader and gull roosts on our side, and gull roosts on sand spits farther up the channel. On winter evenings, the calls of curlews and the *meep-meep* cries of oystercatchers are lonely and haunting in the fading light.

Clonakilty is perhaps 3km (2 miles) away and we are walking towards it. On our left are thickets of sally, alder and gorse, on the right, the sea. A small, decked fishing boat is sometimes dry-berthed here, alongside a shed, festooned in nets. Now, wheel tracks can be discerned along the shore, leading towards the road. We follow the track and reach the tarmacadam causeway at the eastern end of Beamish's Lagoon.

(7) The walk across the causeway to our starting point is just a few hundred metres, the lake on our left, the harbour on the right. Widgeon, teal and mallard may well be seen on the lagoon. Greenshank favour the far margin, roosting in small flocks on the reedy shore. There is a heronry close by and, since egrets have become resident in Ireland, they too are often seen here, pure white, elegant little herons. A Purple Heron – a rare vagrant from Eurasia or Africa – once made the lake its home, attracting hordes of birding 'twitchers'. Look out for unfamiliar species; it is a lake not often 'watched' and there is no reason why such rarities should not turn up again.

RATHBARRY, CASTLEFREKE AND THE LONG STRAND

Key points: Long Strand – mature woods – the tallest memorial cross in Ireland – Rathbarry Castle – ruins of Rathbarry churches – Castlefreke Mansion – Kilkeran Lake and shore – sand dunes – a mile-long storm beach.

Start/finish: the car park at the western end of Long Strand, about 9.5km (6 miles) southwest of Clonakilty, grid ref.: W323346

Distance: 7.2km (4.5 miles).
Map: OSi Sheet 89 **Walking Time:** A leisurely 2.5 to 3 hours

---

(1) I chose a clockwise circuit in order to head into the westering sun on the return. To walk the 1.5km/mile-long stretch of Long Strand as the sun sets over the sea, with black islands and dark headlands silhouetted to the west, is as near a spiritual experience as this worn soul could hope for.

The car park at the western end of Long Strand is separated by the road and the sand dunes from the beach. Behind us is Lough Rahavarrig, the waters of which are almost entirely hidden by reed beds. Some way beyond it, we see the partly restored ruins of Rathbarry Castle, with an orange dwelling house alongside and, farther back, the turrets of Castlefreke. To the right, are the ruined Rathbarry churches.

In summer, nesting reed buntings and sedge warblers may be spotted on Lough Rahavarrig where they perch acrobatically on the reed heads, which are full of seeds. Swallow and martin flocks gather here before autumn migration. Reed beds, with their myriad winged insects, are a last grub-stop for these hirundines before setting off on their 8,000km/5,000-mile trek south.

With the lough on our right, we set off from the car park on a rough path parallel to the road, passing along an old stone wall, colonised by spleenwort, a small, fern-like plant. The path swings right: it is easy to see our route, passing through a picket fence, with a Coillte

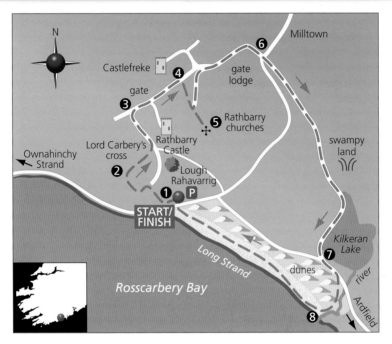

(Irish Forestry) sign welcoming walkers and an arrow directing us up the hill. In season, stands of wayside wild flowers start immediately, bluebells and red campion, ragged robin and foxgloves. But the displays farther along are more spectacular.

To the right is a dead forest, leafless trunks and branches, stark and grey, like something from Tolkien's *The Lord of the Rings* or Cormac McCarthy's *The Road*. Maritime Pines, they are salt-resistant but here the trees nearest the sea have succumbed to wind and weather, or perhaps poor nutrition in the soil. We also encounter both Monterey Cypress (macrocarpa) and Monterey Pines (*Pinus Radiata*) on this walk. Planted exclusively along the coasts of Britain and Ireland, both have a very small natural range, having survived the Ice Age on a single headland in California.

The path climbs steeply, sometimes eroded by winter rains. The

Lord Carbery's cross   Lord Carbery's cross detail

wall of the old Rathbarry estate is on our left behind a screen of sycamores, these apparently unaffected by the salt-bearing south-westerlies. In May, meadow buttercups are mingled with bluebells and carpets of red campions, and with tall, pink-flowering willowherb in summer. Bracken begins to unfurl it's 'shepherds' crooks' in late spring: unlike ferns, it stands on a single stem, with bare areas between the fronds. A seat by the wayside affords fine views.

We reach level ground under big pines where the path divides; incongruously, a small cushion of sea pinks thrives at the base of one tree. There are seats and a fingerpost pointing to 'The High Cross' on the left fork. We take this fork, continuing uphill. Passing through a gap in the old estate wall, we walk along a narrow path. Again, wild flowers galore – yellow pimpernel, stitchwort, germander speedwell and brakes of gorse on the field-side ditch.

(2) The impressive Celtic cross stands on a grassy plateau at the summit of Croghna Hill. Nearby, two simple seats overlook magnificent views to Long Strand and Galley Head. The cross, erected in 1902 by Mary, Lady Carbery, in memory of her husband, Algernon William

George, the 9th Baron, stands 9.5m (30ft) tall and is the highest memorial cross in Ireland. The lettering on the plinth is beautifully designed, drawn from old Irish styles. The front, east-facing shaft rises in seven panels depicting the life of Jesus. The circular headpiece depicts the crucified Christ. On the rear, intricate Celtic knotwork is carved in stone, along with mythical creatures.

Leaving the monument, we cross the grass and take up the track leading downhill. After a short distance, another track, the lower one, joins us from the right. We are soon walking beneath tall Monterey pines. We pass macrocarpas, massive spreading trees, growing to 35m (115ft) tall, with brown, ridged bark, and lemon-scented scale-leaves (like the palms brought to church on Palm Sunday). The cones are small and spherical, with 'plates' rather than 'bumps'. Branches are often wind-broken and some show evidence of this.

The track is wide, in April bordered by Irish spurge, with dark green leaves and pastel green 'flowers'. The sticky, milky sap is toxic; the juice of the *tabiba*, a relation, is still used in the Canary Islands to stun fish in pools. Ferns abound, the delicate lady fern, the more robust male fern, hard fern and hart's-tongue.

Looking east through the trees, we see the ruined Rathbarry churches to the right and, at centre, the ivy-grown ramparts of the first Rathbarry Castle, built on the site of an old fort atop the escarpment. A wall of arches is all that remains of this older structure, built by Randal Oge Barrymore in the fifteenth century, probably on an ancient *dún* fort. It was burnt and pillaged many times, and a tower house and bawn – the 'new' Rathbarry Castle – was built by his descendants. Since the property has passed into new ownership, a dwelling house has been erected in the central area, painted bright orange. Around the new house are the old outbuildings, a courtyard and stables, surrounded by a high stone wall. However, the surrounding artefacts, including the stables and Castlefreke, have been closed to the public in recent years.

The path widens to a forestry road. Where areas have been recently logged, foxgloves, willowherb, pussy willow and occasional pine seedlings have colonised the ground. This is ideal nightjar habitat, but this crepuscular species is now very rare.

As we continue, the light through the tall trees is quite beautiful, beech trees here and there and ivy shining on the forest floor. Some trees are Wellingtonia (Giant Redwoods, Sequoia), tall conifers, with

Castlefreke, under renovation

pendulous branches. The world's largest tree, they may live in their native habitat, California's Sierra Nevada, for up to 3,000 years, attain a height of 80m (262ft) and a weight of 2,000 tonnes. To germinate, the seeds need burnt earth. The bark is rich in tannin, discouraging insects and disease. The forest floor and fallen trunks are mossy. We pass a grove of eucalyptus on the left and then a formidable gate pier capped with an inverted pyramid inlaid with a 'fishbone' of stones.

(3) We emerge onto a tarred estate road via a gap closed to vehicles by a barrier like a barber's pole, painted black and amber. Coillte, the forestry company that manages the woods nearby, has erected a useful plaque with a map and information about the trails, Lord Carbery's cross and the trees. There is a lake in the marshy field opposite, with a circular island, newly constructed, at centre. It is overlooked by Castlefreke mansion, atop a green hill. We walk right, along the road. A laneway leads to Rathbarry Castle on our right, and opposite is a gate carrying a warning that the field beyond is private property. The field climbs a hill with Castlefreke on top, stark against the skyline, presenting a perfect photo opportunity. This is the best view we will get of the mansion.

The towers still wear sleeves of ivy at the time of writing but the house is under extensive renovation with, it seems, all the stonework of the 'battlements' not only cleaned but entirely renewed, and windows replaced. To the east is Galley Head, and the cliffs below it; to the west, large, black islands – High Island, Seal Rock, The Stags and Toe Head.

(4) After viewing Castlefreke across the field, we continue walking right. Some distance along, we must watch out for a gap in the ditch, signposted 'Rathbarry Churches in ruins'. Here, stepping stones cross a small stream to a narrow funeral path with a rushy field on the right and wild currant on the left. The currant bears lovely pink flowers in March but these should not be brought indoors as they smell of ammonia or cat pee. Next, we briefly pass a small bamboo jungle. Beyond the fields on the right, we can see Rathbarry's stables. Here, a broad path joins from the left: we walk straight ahead and after passing under some tall trees, go through a stone stile into the church field.

(5) The most recent of the churches is relatively well preserved, built in 1825 of cut stone, replacing the structure 500 years older alongside it – the difference between the neat cut stone of the new and the rough field-stones of the old is immediately apparent. The tomb of Ralph Freke, who died in 1717, overlies the eastern end of the south wall. The tower has upright pillars, like 'chimneys' at the corners. There is a

Rathbarry Castle

Rathbarry churches

crest above the arched portico, which is roofless. The rear window, of three arches, is extremely elegant, as are the windows to the sides. Beneath it, the wall is inlaid with coloured mosaics, remarkably well preserved, with the legend 'Until He Comes'.

To the right of this church, some walls and the rear gable of the older chapel still stand. Presently, they are being dismantled and the stones stacked alongside for rebuilding, it would seem. Of the many graves, the majority are marked by squat, weather-worn stones standing upright in the grass. There is a single mausoleum, ivy-grown, in the south corner, and a few modern gravestones, one as late as the 1990s. From the raised ground, the Rathbarry complex of stables, castle and house is visible across the fields, and Lough Rahavarrig, southwards.

Returning the way we came, we do not continue to the road but go right at the junction where the side path met ours. This is a wide, green path, with silver birch and Sitka spruce at the sides. After a short time, a Coillte pole barrier is seen, barring vehicle access from the road beyond. (Almost across the road is the Castlefreke car park, with woodland walks behind it. There is no public access to the house.)

As we reach the barrier pole, a narrow path goes right, parallel to the road and we take this. We walk through a strip of cleared woodland, newly planted with spruce and deciduous trees. There is a wealth of wild flowers once again. The path continues inside the road until it turns onto the road at a pretty cut-stone cottage, the former gate lodge.

(6) Passing the gate lodge, we cut straight across the public road and, beside the sign for Ownahincha and Rosscarbery, pass through a stile onto a forestry track alongside a small stream. This is again a Coillte trail. Used by logging machinery, it can be muddy in wet weather.

The trail runs alongside a swamp, with osier trees covered in thick moss, and mop-headed hummocks of Greater Tussock Sedge. Flag irises grow abundantly, with yellow flowers in June. Dragon and damselflies hover over pools. Sometimes, one sees a waterhen – called moorhens in the bird books – skulking about, clucking softly, like a domestic fowl. It is likely that the whole valley was once a sea inlet, with the Atlantic almost washing the walls of Rathbarry Castle. The Lisbon earthquake of 1755 is said to have changed sea levels all along this coast.

After 1.6km (1 mile), the path reaches Kilkeran Lake, once an excellent wild trout fishery but long since polluted with slurry. A few birds are seen: swans, mallard, oystercatchers and redshank, solitary curlews or lapwings in small groups. Clouds of tiny opossum shrimp swim in the shallows. An otter may sometimes be seen.

(7) Crossing the main road, we make our way left, to the southeastern end of Long Strand where the river crosses it to the sea. The river has schools of small mullet in the shallows, sand gobies and dabs. Paths to the beach cross the dunes. In spring and summer, one comes upon mats of colour in the dunes, sandy hollows stippled with orange vetch, purple dog violets, golden trefoil, pink sea bindweed, blue forget-me-nots, all thriving in a sheltered microclimate. Some dunes are 20m (65ft) high, held together by successive layers of marram which, when covered by blown sand, push new shoots up into the light, leaving the roots, in galleries, holding firm the old sand. After rain, one finds glossy black slugs, as long and fleshy as an index finger. Banded snails are common, with brown, purple, bluish and orange whorls. Day-flying moths, like burnets, whose green-and-white caterpillars feed on vetches, and cinnabars, whose black-and-amber striped caterpillars defoliate ragwort, may be seen, and the 'woolly bear' or 'Hairy Molly' caterpillars of buff ermine moths scuttle about on dune paths before they pupate and grow wings.

(8) From the dunes, we emerge onto the huge expanse of the Long Strand, heading away from the river, walking west back to our start point.

Long Strand & Galley Head

SHANNONVALE

Key points: Ballyvahallig Cross Roads – banks of the River Argideen – Civil War memorial – Templebryan Stone Circle – ogham stone and church ruins – Shannonvale Mill – site of 1798 battle – Kilnagross Church – footbridge and ford

Start/finish: Noel Phair's pub at Ballyvahallig Cross Roads, about 3km (2 miles) north of Clonakilty town, grid ref.: W391442

Distance: 6.5km (4 miles)
Map: OSi Sheet 89 **Walking Time:** 3 hours

(1) We set off from the south end of the village, Ballyvahallig Cross Roads, in front of Noel Phair's pub. Here at the crossroads is an area of flowers and grass, named the Noel Phair Memorial Garden, displaying a plaque commemorating a 1798 battle fought just a mile up the road, the only Munster engagement in that unhappy revolt. Twentieth-century reproduction 'standing stones' stand erect around it; we will shortly be seeing the real thing. Opposite is a cottage with a hairy palm tree hung with flower baskets in the garden. We notice the silo of the old mill, rising above the trees in the river valley below. We will visit it later, and give its history then.

We set off walking northwest, on the road opposite the pub, a leafy and pleasant lane, rising slightly as it goes. Soon, the fields on our right fall away to the Argideen, one of the most important sea trout and salmon rivers in Munster. Below the surface, tresses of green weed move in the currents, like Ophelia's hair in the Pre-Raphaelite painting. Its white flowers speckle the surface. Woods rise on the other bank – small copses mark the river's course.

(2) As a substantial farmhouse (painted yellow at the time of writing) comes into view on the opposite bank, we will find a small pathway leading down to the river, perhaps used by anglers. There is a badger sett in the right-hand ditch, halfway down. At the river are the remains

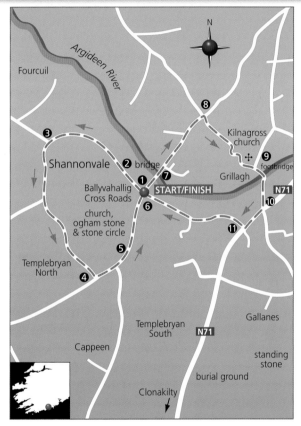

of an old bridge and ford. Water skaters, small, long-legged insects, run on the surface, keeping in equilibrium by constantly forging upstream. On the other side, a leafy path leads towards the village. Birdsong is heard above the gentle rippling of the water. The scene might be from a hundred years ago.

Returning to the road, we turn right, continuing on our route. The last time I passed, there was a herd of pretty cattle in a field, red and shapely as roe deer. This is a great walk for viewing the new cattle that graze the Irish countryside, their diverse hues and strains.

(3) The first turning can be confusing; do not take the 'main' road, veering right, but the road directly ahead, alongside a new house with a stone wall and gate pillars. We pass two more houses a few metres along. This road, which climbs gently, is little used; grass grows down the centre. It presents panoramic views over lovely countryside, with low hills on the eastern horizon. Navelwort, mosses and hard ferns grow on the 'ditches', the word used in Ireland for field walls. We pass a cluster of new houses. Beyond them, on the left, near the ruins of an old stone cottage with a new house nearby, a somewhat novel fountain, utilising an old milk churn suspended from a tree, can be seen in a yard amongst JCBs and forklifts for hire. Opposite, to the right, is a small road; we pass it by. There are wrens and robins in bushes, and, in October, haws everywhere in dense red clumps on the whitethorns, as bright as fuchsia flowers, which are still in bloom. In winter, the haws provide for native birds and for flocks of redwing and fieldfare thrushes that migrate from Russia and Scandinavia.

A farmhouse on the left proudly displays a plaque on its gable, 'Overall Winner, 1993 West Cork Environmental Campaign'. The house has a very pretty frontage, covered in Virginia creeper, rising from a bright green lawn. It is an idyll of a country cott, a dream home urban dwellers would die for.

(4) Downhill, afterwards, to a T-junction, where we turn left, passing through a group of houses, some newly built. We shortly reach another junction, with a 'Yield' sign. Again we go left, passing a memorial cross, a copper shield in a circle. It records, in lovely old Irish script, that one Tadg Ó h-Uallaig, a captain in the 3rd Brigade, Cork IRA, was killed here on 27 March 1921. He was shot dead by a companion, whose gun went off when he was cleaning it. Just beyond the memorial, is a granite plaque inscribed with the name of the village in English and Irish.

Templebryan stone circle in summer

Templebryan pillar stone

(5) The road is wider, now, with a white line down the centre. About 200 yards beyond the cross, on the left, opposite the first house, stones protruding from the stone wall form rudimentary steps enabling access to the field in which stands Templebryan stone circle.

The stone circles, of which County Cork has most in Ireland, were raised as places of worship during the late Bronze Age, *c.* 4,000 years ago. At Templebryan, there are five stones, the tallest of 2.1m (7ft), with a smaller stone in the centre. Jack Roberts, in his *Antiquities of West Cork*, reckons these are half the original number, and that the 'cloch', or stone, from which Clonakilty took its name (*Cloch na Coillte*, 'the Stone of the Wood') is amongst them. The owner of the land generously allows visitors. In the next field north, uphill from the stone circle, an ogham or pillar stone stands in 'a classic early Christian church site consisting of the ruins of the tiny chapel within a circular enclosure' (Roberts). Access may be gained via a gap in the hedge and climbing over the wall.

The tall, slim pillar stone is dramatic against the sky, reminiscent of the obelisks raised in the Sun temples of ancient Egypt. The *Archaeological Inventory of County* Cork identifies it as an ogham stone, that is, a stone bearing ogham markings, but little trace remains of these. A roughly circular 'bullaun' stone, lies on the grass beside it, with a water-filled hollow in the centre. Bullaun stones may have been used as mortars for grinding grain or as baptismal fonts at ancient churches. Legend has it that this stone always holds a few spoonfuls of water even in the driest summer, and that the water level rises and falls with the tides. Also, that the water is effective in curing warts.

Back on the road, we descend, past houses, to the pub cross. Here, we can finish the walk, or continue to the second round of the figure-of-eight, about the same walking distance as the first.

(6) Passing the pub – on the right – we continue straight downhill. The silo of the old Shannonvale Mill stands prominent over the tall trees. We reach the bridge, a lovely spot to pause, with the dark brown river below, and swirls of green weed in the current. Upriver, a small weir murmurs, and trout break the surface of the dark pools under the shadows of the trees. A bed of flowers and shrubs along the verge manifests the pride of Shannonvale's citizens.

(7) We turn right down a lane. On the right, a green lawn, a municipal amenity, runs down to the river. Ahead is the silo and the old mill, stone buildings on right and left, with red brick arches and enormous cut field stones on the corners. 'Danger – keep out', a sign warns but, at the time of writing, a building at the end was open, as if for viewing. If allowed entry, we can see, inside, the ceiling supported by a line of wooden columns, and the fine stonework of the walls.

Shannonvale Mill and village

Garden with model mill and old farm machinery, Shannonvale

Shannonvale Mill was established by the Earl of Shannon in 1760 for the manufacture of linen, and a nearby field, where the linen was laid out, was known as the Bleach Field. Linen weaving was, then, a cottage industry in this part of West Cork, with many home looms supplying 'coarse linen'. In 1790s the mill was burnt down, probably by rebels, known as 'White Boys'. In the 1820s, it was turned into a corn mill.

Returning to the road, we turn right. The neat houses of many colours on the right – pink, terracotta, ochre – were once the homes of mill workers. On the left, at a cottage called 'The Old Mill', is an extraordinary garden, complete with leprechauns, a miniature working model of the watermill, brightly painted model houses and antique farm machinery.

Now out of the village – no shop, one pub – we pass the name sign, *Béal a Mhuí Shailigh*, Shannonvale, and come to a memorial commemorating the Rising of 1798. Here, at 'The Battle of the Big Cross', the principal Munster engagement of 1798 was fought, and lost, under the captaincy of Tadhg O'Donovan Asna on 19 June 1798. He and 100 of his followers were slain in the battle and their bodies later displayed in Clonakilty town.

1798 marble memorial

(8) We take the turning right immediately beyond the monument, a pleasant country road with brakes of lilac and montbretia on the left. It was known as *Bothairín na Foladh*, 'the little road of blood'. The battle moved down this road to the river, leaving many dead. The road descends, crossing the brick humpbacked bridge of the old West Cork railway line and passing through a tunnel of trees. We see, below, the small Church of Ireland church at Kilnagross, with its graveyard, roof bell and round 'sun' window. Fourteen of the 1798 dead are buried here. Amongst fine Celtic crosses may be found the graves of Henry Ford's grandparents – Ford, of the Model T, was born at Ballinascarthy, a few miles away.

(9) Opposite the church, at the mouth of a lane leading to the river, was a *'cillín'*, a burial place for children who died before being baptised. The lane leads down to the west bank of the Argideen and the small

iron footbridge and ford that crosses it. In spring, swallows and martins swoop and hurl over the surface, flitting beneath the footbridge at breakneck speed. About 275m (300 yards) up the leafy lane on the other side, we come to the main Clonakilty–Bandon road.

(10) A wide grass margin inside a fat yellow line gives plenty of safe space for walking. The seamless stream of traffic swishes past. After 90m (100 yards), we leave it behind, turning right at the end of a line of Leyland cypresses. Behind the cypresses are the playing fields of the Clonakilty Rugby Football Club named on a sign by Tomás Tuípear whose signwriting has made the Clonakilty streets amongst the most attractive in West Cork.

(11) The right turning takes us past the entrance to the RFC, with the West Cork Business and Technology Park on our left. It ascends a humpbacked bridge over the old railway route; lengths of old rail track have been recycled as fencing along this stretch of road. The river is below us, on the right, with woods on the other side and the silo of Shannonvale rising above the trees. This is a narrow, high-banked road and, although there is little traffic, care should be taken to stay close to the ditch. Walking back to our starting point, we are heading west into the sun. As the pub comes in sight, the prospect of the village lies below us.

The Argideen from Shannonvale Bridge

ROARINGWATER RIVER WALK

Key points: the Roaringwater River – old stone quays – a McCarthy castle – scenic graveyard – ruins of churches

Start/finish: Meen Bridge on Skibbereen-to-Ballydehob road, about 5km (3 miles) east of Ballydehob, grid ref.: W037350

Distance: 6.5km (4 miles), with an optional extra of 1.5km (1 mile).
Map: OSi Sheet 88 Walking **Time:** 2 to 3 hours

(1) We turn in off the main (N71) Skibbereen-to-Ballydehob road at Aghadown RC church, the Church of the Holy Rosary, crossing the ivied bridge on the old road to reach the car park opposite the imposing church. A new bridge, with less character but more strength, carries the N71 over the river just above it. We walk downriver from here.

Before setting off, a visit to the church is well worthwhile for the beauty of the Sarah Purser windows above the altar, made in 1905, and the rose window above the door, best seen from the choir gallery, made at the Harry Clarke Stained Glass studios in Dublin in 1943.

The small Roaringwater River, for which the huge bay is named, rises 9.7km (6 miles) north, on the slopes of Mount Kid. Going west, the next river that feeds the bay is the Leamawaddra, the 'Dog's Jump' River. 'Dog's Jump Bay' would hardly have had the same resonance. The old name was *Loch Treasna*, Transverse Lake, fine in the Irish, turgid in English. Opposite is Kilcoe National School, built in 1897.

Immediately past the school, there are outcrops of rock covered in gorse and heather. There is hazel on the waterside, and birch and goat willow, all once used for making brooms, baskets and lobster pots. On the stream, pond skaters dash about the surface on splayed legs.

Most of our common wild trees can be found along this lane: hawthorn, blackthorn and holly, alder, ash, hazel, sycamore and small oaks. A robust growth of crinkly grey-white lichen colonises the *sceacs*,

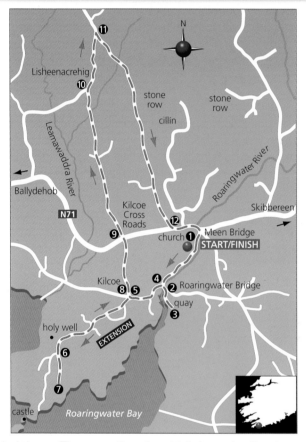

aka blackthorns. The ground is rocky, with little grazing. Foxgloves thrive on the roadside, and primeval-looking polypody ferns. Stonecrop, red in spring, creeps over the rocks, with tiny succulent-type leaves and, later, tiny star-like flowers.

As the road descends with the stream, we are separated from the water by bracken and impenetrable brakes of self-seeded trees, largely willows. A snowberry bush, an American import now gone native, has established itself on the roadside.

Sometimes, the river bank can be accessed. The water rushes over small cataracts and the patterns and colours of the bark of the riverside saplings are beautiful and infinitely varied. In March, the mini-swamps are golden with marsh marigolds, like large buttercups. As we come in view of a white house on the corner, the stream gurgles in a deep gully on our left, perhaps roars (hence the name?) when in flood. Bluebells, and a stand of orchid-like blue flowers, called bugles, speckle the verge. Lime-green hart's-tongue ferns grow in the shadows.

(2) A road rises steeply to the right as we reach the gable of the white house; these days, large gates, with entry phone, front the road, somewhat incongruous in such an idyllic setting. We pass it and cross the small bridge. St Patrick's Cabbage, a Lusitanian species, is to be found on the ditches along this walk, and is worth looking out for.

On the bridge wall opposite, wild strawberry may be found, both barren strawberry and the variety that carries small, sweet fruits.

Mouth of the Leamawaddra River

A short distance after the bridge, we bear right, following the river which now becomes a tidal creek, on our right. Seaweed is in evidence just below the bridge, and large mullet swim up to this point from the sea. Local people tell me otters are regularly seen. The tree-hung bank on the other side would give plenty of cover.

(3) As we round the corner, we come on an idyllic scene, a wide pool of still, brown water, with an old stone quay splashed with the colours of sea pinks, white scurvy grass and the odd prawn pot in spring. Towards the mouth of the inlet, standing alone near the water's edge, is a small, neat corrugated-iron cabin, painted rose, with a blue roof and an object like an inverted cooking pot capping the stovepipe chimney. In April, sea pinks flower between it and the water, and the escarpment behind is bright with gorse. To one side is a stone well, and a track that leads back to the mouths of some small caves in the hillside; these were copper mines. The gated well, beneath the cabin, is still used by local people and apparently folk even arrive from Cork city to enjoy its water, said to have curative powers.

There is much of interest at the quay. Various seaweeds cling to the stone ramparts or grow in the water below, channelled wrack, horned wrack and 'egg wrack', as knotted wrack is sometimes called. The latter can be over a metre long, with leathery branches and egg-shaped air bladders. When it is cast up and dries – as it is here – children enjoy stamping on it. A trawl of these weeds with a stout shrimping net will discover crabs, prawns, sea sticklebacks, pretty two-spot gobies and wonderfully ugly but harmless scorpion fish.

Lovely gardens come down to the quay, one with a magnificent Chilean fire tree, flowering like a giant orange fuchsia in spring. Wild turnip grows in profusion. Ravens nest in the trees opposite; stately herons stalk the shore below the cabin; swans drift near the quays, hoping to be fed. Shelduck, a very beautiful large duck, white, with a striking green-black head, red bill, and chestnut band about the breast, also visit. Unusually, females are dressed as brightly as the males. Because they nest in old rabbit burrows, the female's plumage doesn't have to be sod-brown for camouflage, as with mallard, teal and other ducks. We have seen a stoat here, and various butterflies, including holly blues, painted ladies and, later in the year, red admirals.

We retrace our steps to the house by the bridge. In its gardens, sloping down to the river, Ti trees (*Cordyline Australis*) flourish. Known locally as 'palms', they are natives of Asia and the Pacific isles. They do well in West Cork's Gulf Stream climate.

(4) Rounding the gable of the house, we take the road ascending steeply behind it. It is a pretty, leafy road, with a patch of wetland on the right, dense with flag irises, the fleur-de-lys of France, in bloom in May before we pass a ruined house above it, also on the right. The climb is short. Celandine, germander speedwell – like forget-me-not – primroses, violets and hedge parsnip throng the verges, each in its season. Honeysuckle festoons the trees. We pass the entrance to a house with a long, well-kept lawn, then a vernacular farmhouse and outbuildings with a vernacular manure-heap in the yard.

Almost at the top of the climb, we find, on the left, an ancient graveyard in which stands the remains of Kilcoe's eighteenth-century RC parish church, a single gable, and a few graves marked by Celtic crosses. We pass three churches on this walk, two ruins and one standing, spanning 500 years. The ancient church wall is a veritable rock garden, colonised by spleenwort, navelwort, stonecrop, vetches and hard ferns,

(5) We top the rise 45m (50 yards) along. Mount Gabriel stands dramatically on the skyline ahead. Soon we reach a four-cross roads, and have an optional extension of 2.5km (1.5 miles).

Optional Extension: turning sharp left, we follow the road, ignoring turnings into fields. We shortly see the sea to the west, with Mount Gabriel in the mid-distance. From here, the twin orbs on its summit – like giant golf balls or domes on mosques – are in silhouetted against the sky. They are part of a communications system monitoring air and sea traffic on the North Atlantic. Ballydehob Harbour is seen to the west, with the near sea lined with mussel 'ropes' on the surface, recent phenomena. Across the water to the southeast, we can see Ringcoliskey Castle on Turk Head, built in 1495, a one-time stronghold of the O'Driscolls. The beacon at Baltimore can be seen in the distance, beyond.

(6) The road divides like a Y; we take the left fork and, descending, enjoy close-up views of Roaringwater Bay. Between us and Reen Point, on our right, we see the twin islets, Illaunroemore and Illaunroebeg

Roaringwater River

Kilcoe Castle

('red island', big and small). Cattle graze on the 'beg'. Now, the huge bay and its islands are laid out in front of us, the surface divided with hundreds of mussel lines.

Kilcoe Castle is a magnificent fortified tower house of the McCarthy Riabachs, now the property of the actor Jeremy Irons, who extensively restored it, shading its walls terracotta; tower houses were often painted, it seems. The main tower is of four storeys, the corner tower of six, with dungeons beneath. Built on Mannin Island Beg, now reached by a bridge, it overlooks the larger Mannin island. The road leading to it is private, but we can enjoy a good view from the road above.

(7) At the end of this road, after passing brakes of flowering currant – a garden escape that brightens the hedges of West Cork with pink flowers – we reach the oldest of the three churches at Kilcoe, with a graveyard alongside. This church was already in ruins by 1615. The stone windows are elegant and beautiful, overlooking a rugged and

beautiful view. Ruined walls enclose the burial ground, with lines of low, uninscribed gravestones, weathered and lichen-grown. Inscribed headstones and chest tombs date from the 1860s. Overlooking the bay and islands, few resting places can be as sublime as Kilcoe.

We return to the crossroads. Sometimes, here, in spring, a 'fall' of swallows may suddenly come in off the sea. Swallows are 'site faithful' and find their way back to the barns or eaves where they were reared.

(8) We arrive back at the crossroads, where we earlier turned left to take the extension. Now, we go straight ahead, inland towards the hills, taking up the main route. The roadside fields are scrubby, with gorse and rough gazing.

(9) At Kilcoe Cross Roads, we cross the main N71 – a good view of Ballydehob Bay to the left – and continue up the small road opposite. After passing a timber yard, there is a small, neat Church of Ireland graveyard. A cut-stone vault of the Townsend family – (see Castletownshend and Castlehaven Walk) – is just inside, sealed with a tight-fitting iron gate on the outside of which roost dozens of *petite gris* or common garden snails. These are edible, but never eaten by the Irish. Fine Scots pines edge the site, with singing blackbirds and thrushes on spring evenings.

The road rises and falls in gentle dips. One rarely meets a car. This is a mellow West Cork walk, the quiet road, the bogland, the distant

The hut at Roaringwater Bay quays

hills, the transition from usable land to land that hasn't been changed and is unlikely to ever be. Knockaphukeen ('the fairies' mountain') is almost straight ahead, Mount Gabriel and Mount Corrin off to our left. Topping a rise, we look out on miles of empty hills. A section of the Sheep's Head Way, through Barnageehy ('the windy gap'), is only a few miles north.

(10) We ignore a road to our left and pass Lisheenacrehig, a few farmhouses by the roadside. The green fields begin to give way to rock. Irish spurge, with vivid lemon flowers that look like leaves, blooms everywhere hereabouts in May. Cuckoo flowers grow where the verge is wet; delicate white stitchwort hangs from the ditches. Now relatively close to Mount Gabriel, we can see the scars of the ancient copper mines on its flanks.

(11) Reaching the T-junction, we take a very sharp right, doubling back towards the sea. The woodland skirting the road is silver birch and willow. Once, in early October, I found two fine, largely unwormed birch boletus mushrooms under these trees, with caps big and fat as half Jaffa oranges. There may also be saffron milk caps, another good eating mushroom, under the pines. Some beehives have been sited at the forest edge; presumably gorse, heather, meadowsweet and, possibly, the catkins of birch and willow provide nectar for the bees.

These seemingly barren uplands are host to many butterflies and moths whose caterpillars feed on bog myrtle, whortleberry and bell heather. 'Hairy Mollies' and the furry caterpillars of fox moths cross the road. Their pretty hairs are defensive, deterring predators by sticking in their eyes.

Between rock outcrops, small 'rivers' of grazing grass are vivid green. In boggy places, willows and rushes grow, and tall royal ferns. Bog cotton speckles the fields. Chiffchaffs flit amongst roadside willows, with the occasional robin or wren. Cock stonechats perch on high brambles and sing. I spied a pied flycatcher in May, a blithe newcomer probably en route to inland pastures.

(12) Soon, we reach the N71 again. Turning left, we pass a one-time country post-office-cum-shop and, unless we are thirsty, The Cross House pub. Only a hundred metres away are the bridge and church where we began.

ROSSBRIN HARBOUR AND STOUKE

Key points: sheltered Rossbrin Harbour and quay – Rossbrin Castle – high roads with distant views of Baltimore and beacon – Stouke burial ground – panorama of Roaringwater Bay and the islands.

Start/finish: Rossbrin Quay, grid ref.: V977318

Distance: 6km (3.7 miles)
Map: OSi Sheet 88 *Walking Time:* 2 or 3 hours

---

(1) We set off from Rossbrin Quay, reached by taking the second left turn, signposted Rossbrin Boatyard, off the R592 Ballydehob-to-Schull road, about 1.5km (1 mile) west of Ballydehob. Travelling south towards the sea, the boatyard comes into sight on the right after about 2.5km (1.5 miles). Just before reaching it, we take the sharp left and swing right immediately afterwards. This takes us along the shore to the small stone quay where we begin, with the castle directly opposite, across the water. If we pass the boatyard, we will arrive at the slip, not the quay.

From the quay, we head east, with the water on our right. Once I saw a seal hunting here – a female or immature grey, with the grey's distinctive sloped forehead. The water was no more than a metre deep and when she dived, one could clearly follow her progress underwater. Mullet swirled and jumped in the shallows as she approached.

The O'Mahony castle, Rossbrin Castle, a rectangular tower on a rock outcrop at the west side of Rossbrin Bay, was reputedly built in 1310, but the surviving remains are of fifteenth- or sixteenth-century origin. Once a centre of learning under Finghin O'Mahony, 'the scholar prince of Rossbrin', it was abandoned in the early seventeenth century, after the Irish–Spanish defeat at the Battle of Kinsale. The remains stand to four storeys on the northeast corner, like a finger pointing at the sky.

Sea pinks sprout from fissures between the stone blocks of the pier, and scurvy grass, with small white flowers, grows in mats along the edge. How convenient that it grew so close to the sea, this important

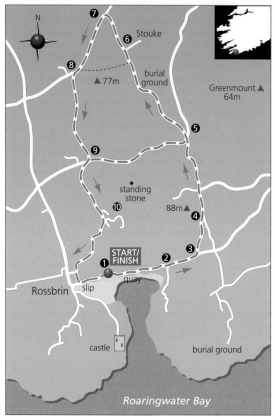

source of vitamin C for old-time sailors facing long voyages and scurvy which, at best, rotted their gums, at worst, took their lives.

Seaweeds, in long trails, float on the surface, buoyed by their 'bubbles', which carry the fronds up to the light as the tide rises. Knotted wrack is most common but spiral and channelled wrack grow in abundance. These shallow water algaes are an ideal habitat for 15cm/6-inch-long, fifteen-spined 'sea' sticklebacks. Rarely seen but easy to catch with a net, they are best not disturbed in summer, when 'nesting'.

Sea Pinks

Bluebells grow on the landward verge in spring. A few lovely houses are set back from the road, fronted by gracious lawns. Outside them are clumps of libertia, a New Zealand flower, their tall spears covered in white flowers. Between us and the water, small fuchsias and whitethorns edge the lane. The dark green grass is peppered with white stitchwort. The calm water reflects the old stone walls, dappled with orange lichen, which edge the eastern shore.

In springtime, 'wild garlic' grows in profusion before we come to the small pebble beach at the eastern end, its oniony odour distinctive as we pass. In May, it is a lovely sight on the Irish roadside, with white flowers and three-cornered stems (it is sometimes called 'three-cornered garlic'). However, farmers fear it – if cows eat it, it taints the milk.

In the field ahead, red-brown rabbits hop about on summer evenings. A small, gurgling stream pours from the under the honeysuckle on a ditch on our left. The pebble beach is worth a ten-minute pause. For the children, there is much dried 'egg wrack' to pop. The rocks are splattered with orange lichen, bright as the yolk of seagull eggs. Pinks, scurvy grass and large, glossy-leafed sea beet grow here, the latter, a relative of beetroot and sugar beet, is one of the few plants that can survive salt spray.

Amongst other specialist plants of the seashore, moss campion and rock sea spurrey root on nearby walls and rocks.

(2) As we leave the sea, a gate on our right is imaginatively and patriotically decorated with metal net balls atop metal pillars, the whole painted green, white and yellow, Ireland's colours, slightly fading and rusting from the salt air.

Spurge grows profusely on the roadside, with pines on the left, and gunnera, giant 'wild rhubarb', outside a house. The road climbs now, grass growing down the middle.

Rossbrin Castle

(3) We take the first left (where '32' is printed on the OS map). The climb, for a few hundred metres, is quite steep. Behind us, are marvellous views, Rossbrin Castle, and Castle Island behind it, with the gables of ruined houses against the sky. Other islands are the Calf Island group, low on the sea. At the top of this stretch, Baltimore Harbour comes into view to the east, with the white beacon opposite Sherkin Pier shining in the sun. We are on a small back road, now, a dusty boreen.

(4) A road joins from the right and merges into our route. Gorse and heather come down to the roadside. We top a rise with extensive views north and east and, as we pass a 'crossroads' (the left junction, a cattle grid, with big gates, leads only to a farm) we continue straight ahead, going down, heading towards the rolling hills in the distance. In early June, foxgloves are in full flower along the ditch, reaching almost 2m (6.5ft) tall in good years. The fields are scrubby, with white reeds in the lowland bogs. The green of grass, the white of reeds, the gold of gorse are like an Irish tricolour laid across the land.

(5) We now come to a four-cross roads, (where the latitude '33' is printed on the OS map), and go straight through, taking the small road going northwest, keeping to the higher land. (As will be obvious from the map, the road to our left cuts across the 'A' shape of our route and takes us to (9), offering a shorter loop back to base.)

Continuing on the road toward the apex of the 'A', we immediately pass a large rock in a field on the left, with ivy growing up it from a single, thick stem, splaying out, like a one-dimensional tree. The road climbs higher, a quiet road, grass growing up the middle. Now, we have a wonderful view of Mount Gabriel, the twin 'golf balls' of the communications stations on top. In spring, the hedge of berberis

Old postbox, Rossbrin

Stouke burial ground

outside a house on our right is dark green, with prickly, holly-like leaves and little orange flowers, contrasting with the robust yellow gorse growing through it. The road rises, at times as if making straight for Mount Gabriel 6.5km (4 miles) away. Reaching a 'summit', it starts downhill.

(6) Soon we find the burial gound on our right, entered by a small gate. Inside, are old graves, especially towards the back, many of them unmarked. There is a bullaun stone in the south east corner. Bullaun stones may have been primitive mortars for grinding grain or baptismal fonts at ancient churches, where they are often found. The graveyard is still in occasional use. An impressive rhododendron thrives near the back wall.

Leaving the graveyard, we continue our route. The first left turning, marked on the OS map, is a private entrance, a farm path leading to a house.

(7) We continue to the T-junction (the apex of the 'A') and go left, now heading south, towards the sea. We immediately pass a house on the right with the legend, 'Upper Crust Bakery' on the gable. The unpaved farm path mentioned above emerges on our left.

(8) We walk past the bakery and continue until we see a bungalow behind a hedge on the right with a road opposite it, going left, uphill. We take this. Grass grows down the centre and it appears to ascend to the sky. A hundred metres up this road, we reach its summit and a huge vista of Roaringwater Bay, due south, opens before us. Outstanding are the three flat Calf Islands and, beyond them, 10km (6.2 miles) to sea, the high bulk of Cape Clear Island with isolated houses on its slopes.

A farmhouse and its yard straddles the road. The road, given occasional humps and dips, is descending to the sea. Soon, we get glimpses of yacht masts in the boatyard below. The fields on either side are rough grazing, grassy terraces with rocky outcrops. Furze blooms in the small fields, and goat willow and sally. Royal ferns thrive along the verges: these are our most majestic fern, over 1m (3ft) tall, sometimes as tall as 2m (7ft). When the evening sun strikes them, they appear to be golden: perhaps hence the name. In spring, linnets, small brown birds, sing as we pass.

(9) We come to the four-cross roads, with a bungalow visible on the road going left. We go straight across and shortly pass a large house on the left, with well-kept outhouses on the right and a big, half corrugated-iron barn.

(10) Now, a three-cross-roads junction with a dense line of leylandii (Leyland Cypresses) ahead. Here, we turn right and as we go steeply downhill, enjoy breathtaking views over Horse Island and Castle Island, west of it, with its castle down by the water. A channel separates them, with the low-lying Dereen Rocks between. Looking westwards across the land, we can see Mount Gabriel in the distance, with the light catching the twin communication domes on the summit.

In March, the low-growing, pretty yellow flowers of the lesser celandine are common on the roadside – followed, in April and May, by goldilocks and meadow buttercups growing very tall to clear the grass heads when they flower. Celandine is the first of the spring flowers and possibly the best known.

The road descends steeply. The O'Mahony castle is straight ahead, perfectly framed in the view and we can see an area of the harbour close to the quay. Our route hairpins around to the right and here, indeed, is a photo opportunity; the vista must be amongst the best in West Cork. The island immediately 'behind' the castle is Horse Island; we can clearly see the pier and its old grey houses blending perfectly into the landscape. Beyond, are the 'outer islands', and beyond them, the great bulk of *Oileán Cléire*, Irish-speaking Cape Clear Island, the highest – some say the biggest, notwithstanding Sherkin – in Roaringwater Bay.

The lane we walk is leafy and pleasant. We pass through a tunnel of trees, mainly sycamores, with a big red barn on our left, and some whitewashed stone buildings, with red tin roofs. In a field to our right are two stone-built posts, like massive gateposts, the remains of old quarry workings. On the right are tall grasses – libertia, again, with white flowers. In April, there are wild bluebells on the left.

Across a field, on the 'main' road, we see the old National School, painted pink. Built in 1909, it served locals and islanders until it was closed in the 1960s. We come to a 'Road narrows' sign, and a sign indicating a snaking piece of road. Now, back at sea level, we round a stone wall and pass between two quaint old buildings, one on either side of the road. One was a shop for the islanders, run by an old lady who died, aged ninety, only a few years ago. To our right, is the old boat slip, with a low, rusted barge which has decayed into it, seemingly melding with the stone. The boatyard behind us was started in 1993 by a German couple, dry-docking pleasure craft – as many as eighty – in winter, and carrying out maintenance and repairs.

From here, the quay where we began is just a few minutes along the waterside. It is always tempting to linger awhile on the pier before leaving. Rossbrin is a hard spot to leave.

Rossbrin Castle and islands of Roaringwater Bay

LETTER AND BARNANCLEEVE GAP

> **Key points:** the hills above Schull – an old 'green' road – silence and solitude – bog hole life – prehistoric copper mines – magnificent views

Start/Finish: grid ref.: V953345, about 3.2km (2 miles) north of Schull

---

Map: OSi Sheet 88
Distance: 8km (5 miles) **Walking Time:** 2 to 3 hours

The starting point can most easily be reached by turning north, towards the hills, off the main Ballydehob-to-Schull road, approximately halfway between the two towns. The turning is signposted 'Derryconnell House'. Pass Derryconnell House (a B&B, but the sign may not be displayed in off-season; look out for the gantry on which it hangs). Immediately beyond it, the narrow road climbs around a curve, under tall trees, some of them pines. We continue to the top of the rise, ignoring the entrance to a house on the right. The road now descends. On the right, almost hidden behind an escalonia hedge, is an old-fashioned house with a two-pot chimney and, 45m (50 yards) beyond it, a concrete, slate-roofed hut, a pumping station, with a sign outside announcing 'This project is funded under the Clár Programme'. Beside it a green roadway leads to the hills. We set out along it.

(1) The green road on which we set out for Letter – *leitir*, meaning 'wet hillside' – has a gate at the entrance. We will encounter three gates on this route. Care should be taken to ensure that they are left as found. Also, walkers should take care to avoid the animals, especially when there are calves or lambs, and to keep dogs well in control.
    This path is probably very old. It leads from nowhere to nowhere now but once there was a hill fort on the west side, and the name was 'Leitir an Lis', 'hillside of the fort'. There were ancient copper mines (thought to be worked in 1500 BC) and barytes mines close by, and

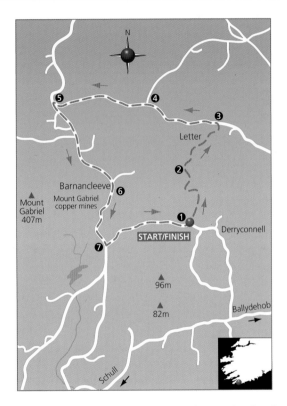

the shafts can still be found. A red circle signifying a ring fort is marked on the map. However, the path, traced by a broken line, is virtually impassable.

If you walk this route in May, listen for the cuckoo. Hereabouts, it is likely to be seeking meadow pipits as surrogates, and the eggs the female cuckoo lays will resemble these in colour, if not in size. Only the male sings 'cuck-oo'. The female chuckles, perhaps because evolution has relieved her of housekeeping.

As we walk between the flat fields of rough grazing, the silence is, at once, noticeable. One may hear the harsh croak of a raven, or

On the green road to Letter

the thrill of a lark high above. Larks are easily identified by their habit of climbing the sky so high as to almost disappear from sight and, circling there, filling the air with song. Ravens are holding their own, at least in West Cork where they are fairly common, nesting in coastal and inland cliffs, and tree hollows. The largest of our crows, they are slightly bigger than rooks from which they are distinguished by their heavy, all-black bill and glossy plumage.

We cross a brown stream at another gate. The surface, and that of most bog pools we will encounter, is often alive with whirligig beetles and pond skaters. Try drumming lightly on the surface with the tip of a bog rush. Beetles will whizz or skate across the surface to it, expecting a drowning fly and a free lunch.

Foxgloves grow along the edge of the stream, a tall, impressive plant with many flowers like purple finger-stalls, much frequented by bumblebees. A few blackthorn bushes grow nearby in this tree-less landscape. When a tree is covered with ivy, hundreds of drone flies and hover flies feed on the green ivy buds in the sun, setting up a melodious hum when disturbed.

The path swings left and then right and climbs gently. Roaringwater Bay, behind us, can now be seen, and Cape Clear Island. As we climb, the Fastnet Rock, 16km (10 miles) due south, is visible; to the southeast, we can see the beacon at Baltimore; and Baltimore village itself, famous for its sailing club and a raid by Algerian pirates in 1631. Gorse bushes, the spiky limbs so thick with flower that they look like yellow bottle brushes, brighten the hillside. Gorse – also known as furze or whins – blooms all year, although less so in winter. This habit inspired a cute old saw to the effect that 'Kissing is out of season when gorse is out of bloom. . .' Western gorse, a smaller variety, and bell heather blanket the ground between rock outcrops, making diversions from the path a prickly business.

Besides whirligigs, small bog holes support lesser water boatmen, which swim on top and scavenge on the bottom. Their cousins, the greater water boatmen, swim upside down and have a vicious beak to which I can attest. Greater water boatmen will prey on tadpoles which may be found hereabouts in wayside drains. Unslurried and unsullied, landscapes like this still provide healthy habitat for the common frog.

(2) We reach the highest point of the green road. Ahead of us, the land falls away and then, in the near distance, rises again to hills with brown slopes of bracken, green conifer plantations, and golden breaks of gorse. To the northwest, we see the high mountains of Kerry beyond Dunmanus and even Bantry Bay. The mountain straight ahead has a

Mountain sheep, Barnancleeve

Cape Clear and the Calf Islands from Barnancleeve

cairn of stones on top. Between us and it, the landscape is sparsely populated; there are no more than ten houses, some almost obscured by trees. As we follow the old road down, Mount Gabriel is to our extreme left, high above.

We reach the first few trees, hawthorns and blackthorns, or *sceacs* as locally known, a rough word for a tough tree. They are gnarled and wind-bent by the prevailing southwesterlies. Evidence of the weathering effect of these can be seen where the rock outcrops are roughly flat on top. Grooves run in a northeasterly direction across the surface, all parallel, made by rain driven by the southwest wind.

There are ruins of stone houses on the left, and a copse of trees ahead. We arrive at the third and last gate.

We pass a large, neat farmhouse on the right and, to the left, there are old buildings, the ancient stone walls beautifully patterned with lichens. Now, the road is paved and we pass three whitewashed out-houses, with red-oxide-painted doors and tin roofs, and a nice garden where butterflies flit over the buddleia. An escalonia hedge and then a stone wall, the stones placed vertically, in the Irish fashion. Brambles have found a hold, and fuchsia; this humble wall supports a diversity of plant species which could while away an hour of investigation. There is tormentil, with red stems and small yellow flowers, also maidenhair spleenwort, hard fern, wall rue, buckler fern, hart's-tongue fern and polypody. Mosses thrive in thick green cushions, wall pennywort sends up stalks of bell-shaped flowers like tiny foxgloves.

(3) At the end of the lane, we reach the narrow main road and turn left. In October, the whitethorn bushes are red with shining haws, the blackthorns purple with sloes. We pass red barns on the left and, some minutes farther on, a cottage. It is a poetic location, with peace in abundance and wild, stark scenery.

We are now walking due west; Mount Gabriel is, at times, dead ahead. A stream a few metres wide crosses under the road; willow and alder grow along it. Alder is typical along most Irish watercourses, a deciduous tree which has, unusually, evolved a small 'cone' which falls and floats downstream and seeds along the banks. Siskins, pretty, yellow finches, often feast on alder catkins in winter, hanging upside down as they feed.

(4) We ignore a road to the right, going north. Bogland is to our left, and also to our right, at times. Tussock Sedge and soft rush grows in the wet places; where there is rock showing; bell heather and western dwarf gorse often colonise the fissures. The road is straight and treeless, although there are the usual small willows and bog myrtle. It is a hot road on a warm day.

(5) Arriving at a T-junction, the main Schull–Durrus road, we turn left. There is a house on our right, with some leylandii trees and, on the other side of the 'main' road, a house across the field with pines lining the driveway.

As we walk south – climbing gently towards the gap at Barnancleeve – the land below us on the left is trenched and ploughed for forestation. Beyond the rushy fields are views to rolling hills. Fuchsia bushes verge the roadside here and there, and on the left are small trees, hazel, blackthorn, whitethorn and, especially, birch. The road continues to rise gently, giving wider and wider views.

(6) The cleft between Mount Gabriel and the hill opposite is a small gorge, worn by weather – Barnancleeve, probably from *Bearna an Chliabh*, a 'basket-shaped gap'. We pass the entrance to a house on

the right and, as we top the rise, come upon a spectacular view. The road clings to the Mount Gabriel side, where the escarpment is steep, as in a 'cutting'. Roaringwater Bay and many of its islands – said to number 365, one for each day of the year – lie spread out below us, an awe-inspiring sight. The largest fully in view is Cape Clear Island, the smallest – and most dramatic – the Fastnet Rock.

The Fastnet Rock, *Carraig Aonair* ('the solitary rock') in Irish, has had a sea light since 1853, with the present lighthouse built in 1904. Until 1989, four lighthouse men lived on the rock, where tides rise 3.6m (12 feet) and currents can run at 3 knots. On only a dozen tides a year is the water calm enough to allow a boat to pull alongside.

In the past, a fanciful local myth said that on May Day the Fastnet went west to Kerry to meet its relations, The Bull, The Cow and the Calf, islands off the tip of Beara, but that since the lighthouse was built it could no longer do so, being pinned down with steel.

Along the roadside, St Patrick's Cabbage, *Saxifraga spathularis Brot*, a Lusitanian species, grows in a profusion I have seen nowhere else. The roadside and the slopes of the gully below are, literally, carpeted in this rare plant, largely confined to West Cork and Kerry, one of fifteen Irish plants that do not grow in Britain.

In the gap, the rock faces are hosts to healthy lichens, an indication of the pure quality of the air. On the west-facing vertical face is a prehistoric copper mine, another at the south end, penetrating some 5m (16ft), with an entrance about 1m (3ft) high. A stone maul – hammer – was found here. Goat willow thrives in the deep watercourse below the road, . Above it, humps of bare rock 'flow' down the hillside, divided by 'streams' of vegetation and cross-hatched

Cuckoo flower   *Barnancleeve Gap with St Patrick's Cabbage*

with fissures, in which heather and scutch grass grow. Behind us are hills behind hills, the blue hills of Kerry in the distance.

We start downhill, the road visible below us almost all the way to Schull. Far off to our left, we can see part of the village of Baltimore, its beacon gleaming white in sunlight, visible to the naked eye on clear days. A variety of butterflies forage on the wild flowers, thistles and fuchsia in this upland country; in early spring, I've seen painted ladies from North Africa, peacocks, and tortoiseshells, and many red admirals later in the year. Willows with reddish branches and white downy buds hang over the roadside ditches, in springtime blanketed in whortleberry with globular flowers like small red currants or tiny Chinese-lanterns. The twin 'humpbacks' of Cape Clear Island stand large and high 9.5km (6 miles) out in the bay – a ferry plies to the islands from Schull Pier. Basking sharks, porpoises, dolphins, even migrating whales, are regularly seen in these waters.

In May and June, the roadside is purple with foxgloves, beautiful but poisonous flowers, the original source of digitalis, effective in the treatment of heart complaints.

(7) About 1km (0.6 miles) below the gap, we see Scots pines ahead, and a white house with two chimneys. Here, we turn left, passing two stone-faced houses. An old house on the right has a tin roof.

A fuchsia hedge edges the road for a long way, on the right. A house surrounded by trees is called Gabriel's Cottage; it has an attractive wooden garden house. The road is undulating, a lonely road in the fastness of the hills. The fuchsia gives out, and there are no ditches or walls on either side, only a few straggling fence posts. Dwarf gorse and bell heather cling to the rocks in the boggy fields, colonised by huge royal ferns, and speckled with the white 'bunny tails' of bog cotton. Pipits fly twittering from rock to rock, and a raven cries harshly overhead.

It was mid-May when I last walked this route; bright yellow tormentil and white cuckoo flowers grew amongst the roadside rushes. As I neared the 'last' house where I began, I heard the cuckoo, and looked for it in the empty hills and bogs around me. With the haunting voice in the distance and the absence of time in the landscape, the earth indeed appeared to be 'an insubstantial, faery place' as William Wordsworth put it. It worked magic for Wordsworth and it worked magic for me.

LONG ISLAND WALK

Start/finish: Midland Pier, where the ferry comes in, grid ref.: V918285

Distance: 6.5km (4 miles)
Map: OSi Sheet 88 **Walking time:** 1.5 hours

Location, access and island life.

Long Island, *Inis Fada*, is located on the north side of Roaringwater Bay, opposite the townland of Colla, 3km (2 miles) south of Schull on the road following the coast. The island population numbers ten but some of the cottages have been renovated and attract visitors in summer. The ferry to Long Island leaves from Colla Pier three time a day at the time of writing (see ferry and cable-car timetables); the passage takes only ten minutes. The island is 4km (2.3 miles) long, by less than 1km (0.5 miles) wide.

Long Island is only a few miles down the road from the popular West Cork town of Schull, but it is a universe away. At Colla Pier, in view of the island, holidaymakers bathe, mess about in small boats and troll for mackerel from the rocks in summer. Colla serves Midland Pier, across the channel, and the two townlands have long been connected. At one time, farmers swam cattle back and forth behind their boats.

On the coast ahead is *Cuas an Mhuillin*, a small inlet with a rock behind it from which 'curative water' is said to issue. People come from all over County Cork to collect it. Also, near Midland Pier, halfway between the small beach and the rock platforms, there is a deep cave. It runs a distance into the island, far beyond the reach of natural light. Danny Murphy, the ferryman, might point it out. Clearly, care should be taken not to enter it when the tide is rising

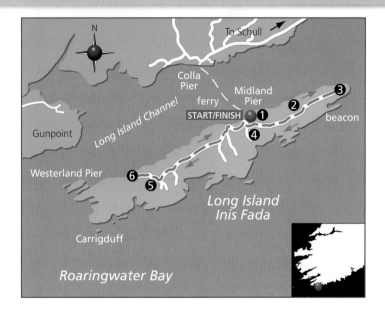

(1) After disembarking at Midland Pier, we follow the road left to walk to the island's easternmost point and the beacon looking out on Castle Island. We pass a few small, neat houses, all of the same design, even to the extensions which have sometimes been added. Some are freshly whitewashed, and look newly built. In fact, they are examples of a type of slate-roofed house built by the Congested Districts Board on many of the Irish islands in 1928; the old houses had sod roofs. Twenty-six such dwellings were built on Long Island. Some have been renovated as holiday homes. Families with a dozen children or more once lived in them.

Grass grows up the middle of the narrow road, which swings around to the right before running more or less straight down the backbone of the island. Irish dwarf gorse has colonised the rocky fields, and the stone walls are colonised with wall pennywort, white foxgloves, and stonecrop. We also meet the usual foreign colonists – originally 'escapees' from (probably mainland) gardens – montbretia, from France and fuchsia, originally from Chile but now naturalised all

The pier on Long Island   *Long Island, typical house*

over Ireland's southwest. Fuchsia is ubiquitous enough to have an Irish name, *Deora Dé*, meaning God's Tears, possibly associating the bright red flowers with Christ crucified. It is used as a shelter belt around some of the isolated houses.

But for wheel tracks by the ditches, the narrow road would be a long field. Here and there, we come upon cars which are not in the best of condition; in fact, some seem to have been immobile for years.

In summer, the land is gold with gorse and purple with heather. Swallows spin in the sky overhead and skim the fields. A leisurely heron rises like a wind-blown umbrella from a nearby hill – an unusual roost for a heron – and a pair of unleisurely snipe rocket from a roadside wetland and zigzag into the sky. Stonechats flit from briar to briar and a cock linnet sings from a post. Yellow flag irises stand tall and bright in a marshy field.

(2) As we pass through a cutting and ascend to higher ground, the views are magnificent, Clear Island to the south, Sherkin, seen over the low-lying Calf Islands, to the southeast, then Baltimore town, with the Napoleonic-era signal tower on the hills above. In the sea far to the west, the Fastnet Rock and its lighthouse, stands lonely and shining in the sun. In Irish, it is called *Carraig Aonair*, 'the solitary rock', surely more appropriate than Fastnet, (from the Viking name) although it was so written on late

medieval Italian charts. The fence posts and roadside stone walls are botanical gardens of lichens. Shortly, we pass a ruin resplendent with orange *Xanathoria*. A lichen associated with the shore, sea ivory, like wisps of stiff, grey-green hair, also thrives on Long Island stones.

The beacon at the end of Long Island, marking the entrance to Schull Harbour, can be seen ahead. In the island peace, the huge communication domes shining atop Mount Gabriel are like artefacts on another planet.

We come upon a tall post fixed upright in the ditch on the right side of the road, riddled with holes which might have been made by ship worms, or teredo worms, and with a large carbuncle three-quarters of the way up; it is a dramatic piece of natural sculpture. Opposite, beyond some marshy fields, is an upright stone, perhaps an ancient standing stone or perhaps simply a scratching post for cattle; there is no one to ask.

(3) As we approach the beacon, the road narrows to a lane, overgrown, and muddy in wet weather. At the time of writing, there is a 'Duty of Care' notice on an entrance, indicating that the land beyond is private. Locals have told me that they themselves and visitors have always walked out to the beacon.

We walk over trackless, open ground just above the rock platforms, which are covered with impressive lichens. There are fallen walls and loose rocks here and there, and a small pond below us, edged by luxuriant royal fern, our most majestic native fern, sometimes achieving heights of 2m (7ft). We are looking out at Castle Island.

We cross a stream above a small, sheltered cove, and continue through a stile, which looks like a sheep gap, onto a field above. Below us, a large, black rock lies offshore across a channel of water as clear as an aquarium, a pristine marine environment, with shellfish and anemones, and long, brown eel grass moving in the flow. Between us and Clear Island, the three Calf Islands lie low on the sea, with ruins of houses visible. Settlements survived on the Calf Islands until the mid-twentieth century, despite the inhospitality of the location, often cut off for weeks in winter storms.

Pink tussocks of sea thrift brighten the black rocks in June. From the beacon, we can see the ruined O'Mahony tower house at the eastern end of Castle Island. It stands on a promontory over the main landing place, probably on the site of an earlier fort.

(4) Retracing our steps, we pass Midland Pier and turn left for Westerland, on what the previous ferryman, John Shelley, once described to us as 'a nice tidy "*slachtmhar*" walk, where you can keep your shoes clean . . .'

We pass some ruined houses, and an old pump on the right; the handle works but no water arrives. The road climbs slightly uphill and past a hundred metres of exposed rock face, which, for a student of lichens, would provide hours of interest. Stonecrop, maidenhair spleenwort and black spleenwort are amongst the many plants that colonise the rocks.

We pass the island school, now converted to a dwelling, and we can see Coney Island to the right, not far offshore, with a nice house on it and a pretty cove. There are some green fields ahead, to right and left of the road as it goes down into a dip. When we reach the rise beyond, we see the Goat Islands, high out of the water.

Across the sound, on our right, Mount Gabriel is large against the sky, with the cleft of Barnancleeve Gap on its right shoulder. Four thousand years ago, paths crossed the mountain to reach the workings on its slopes, the first copper mines in Western Europe. These paths are long since subsumed beneath the brown blanket of bog but, without doubt, the gap would have been one of the routes. Nowadays, it carries the road from Schull to Durrus and from here, so far away, we can see the windscreens of cars going through it flashing in the sun.

(5) We now approach the houses clustered above Westerland Pier, about fifteen in all, many in ruins. The views are very beautiful, and dramatic. A steep-sided channel separates the two Goat Islands, with a tower on Goat Island Little, on the left. The steep-sided channel between them is a dramatic sight.

We reach a T-junction, and the land ahead is uncultivated, rock-rent and 'bockety', with more gorse than grazing. What appear to be two low towers are silhouetted against the western sea; they are the ruined gables of long-abandoned houses. Around them relics of old potato ridges extend down to the very rocks of the shore. This land offered little sustenance, and that little, hard won. Of food for the spirit there was a feast, and if the native people could have lived on the scenery, their bellies would have indeed been filled. Here, like the sea or sky, the land is nature's domain and humans pass but leave little

Left: gall wasps probably caused this strange excrescence on the living tree; middle: lichens; right: the strand at the West End

trace of their having been. The moorland and bog stretch like a brown mantle to the sea: in winter, it is as drab as sackcloth, in summer, purple with heather and golden with gorse. The ferryman said Westerland was a place of great spiritual force, and it is not hard to believe him. There is a power and majesty in the empty land, the sea and sky, and Ireland seems a smaller place, close by but infinitely remote.

(6) We turn right, down to the beach and Westerland Pier. The small strand is a lonely but lovely place, and some rare plants colonise the shingle. The horned poppy is one; its bright yellow flowers may be found as late as October. Little Robin, a member of the geranium family, also grows here. It is very like the often-seen Herb Robert but taller and greener and with smaller flowers. It is very rare, present elsewhere in Ireland only on old walls around Cork city. John Akeroyd's book of island flora says it may not be an Irish native and, in the case of Long, may have been introduced centuries ago. It sometimes grows almost prostrate along the shingle.

Looking out over the land, where any trace of fields has long been subsumed by furze and heather, there is not a single human artefact to snare one in time. A few hours' walking on Long is like a holiday from the world and its business. One wonders if one ever wants to set foot on the mainland again.

CASTLETOWNSHEND
AND CASTLEHAVEN

Key points: unusual village – Bronze Age fort – literary graves – wild places

Start/finish: the car park opposite St Barrahane's RC church, grid ref.: W170315

Distance: 7.5km (4.5 miles) or 10km (6 miles) including extensions
Map: OSi Sheet 89 **Walking Time:** 3 or 4 hours

(1) We begin at the car park opposite the fine, plain St Barrahane's RC church, about 1.5km (1 mile) before Castletownshend on the R595 Skibbereen–Castletownshend road. Hitching rings for Mass-goers' horses are set in the stone wall. The long stone building with the white cornerstones just up the road is Castlehaven National school, built in 1889; the derelict building opposite is the old village hall.

The fields opposite the church are like rivers of green grass pouring down the hill, with islets of rock and gorse dividing them. These rise to gorse-covered outcrops on the skyline. Three thin pillars are silhouetted against the sky, more like tall fence posts than pillars of stone. The remains of a stone row, they are dramatic on our left as we walk down the road.

A stream runs below the church, with brakes of alder and a small marsh. The road is in a boggy dip; spike rushes edge the verge. Above the bend ahead, a flight of walled, stone steps climbs the slope on the other side of a field to one of the finest restored stone forts in West Cork. We ignore the right turning before the bend and continue walking as close to the ditch as possible: this is a somewhat dangerous road and walkers should proceed in single file, with caution.

(2) We reach a gate that says 'No parking' and a fingerpost indicating the fort. A green road stretches beyond it; the grass is regularly mown and the way is maintained. We enter through the gate. Wood violets, primroses, foxgloves and tormentil all occur along the ditches. We

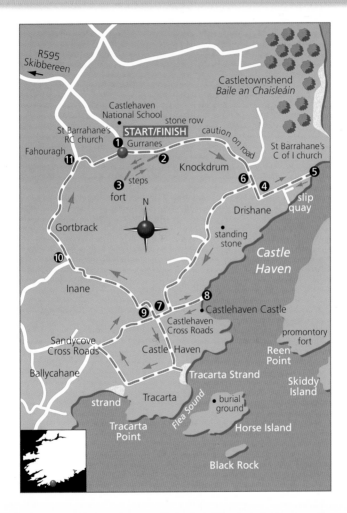

reach the steps; above, the round shape of the low fortress walls can be seen against the skyline. The steps are thoughtfully made, with a 'landing' every so often; they are some eighty in all. At the top, we pass an iron wicket and a piece of field, and arrive at the fort.

Horse Island from Knockdrum   *Castletownshend Castle and pier*

(3) One is immediately taken by the view. Ahead and below, we have a 180° panorama of sky, sea and islands; behind, 180° of undulating landscape, rising to blue, distant hills. There can be few finer lookouts in Munster; on a clear day, we can see as far as Hungry Hill on the Beara Peninsula, and the MacGillycuddy's Reeks near Killarney.

Knockdrum, as the fort is called, is a national monument. Bronze Age, perhaps 3,000 to 4,000 years old, it was part-rebuilt in the mid-nineteenth century and is wonderfully preserved; there are five other ring forts in the compass of this walk but none compares. Boyle Somerville excavated and wrote about it in the 1930s. The walls, over 1.5m (5ft) high, are 2.4m (8ft) across and provide a walkway around the perimeter, which is all of twenty paces in interior diameter and unbroken but for the entrance, at which there is a low 'sentry house'. Inside, is a hut site, without a roof, and a souterrain tunnelled into the bedrock. It is said that Knockdrum was used through the ages as a lookout point for invaders. What a perch!

Below, is a small brown lake; beyond it, the cliffs and Horse Island, flat, with a beach facing the mainland, cliffs at one end, fields divided by stone walls, a ruined house and sheep grazing. To the east, the entrance to Castlehaven Bay, with a white beacon marking Reen Point on the eastern shore. Over the back of Reen, we can see Blind Harbour, the causeway to Myross and the trapped water between it and Squince

Harbour, a sea lake. Offshore, is Seal Rock, Low Island and then High Island, with a crescent of impressive cliffs. The headland in the distance is Galley Head, with lighthouse; the western headland is Scullane Point.

Outside the fort entrance lies a recumbent rock, decorated with cup marks. These sometimes appear on standing stones. Their significance is elusive; they may have been miners' marks, astronomical symbols, plans for hut settlements or, simply, artistic doodles.

At the bottom of the steps, we turn right and retrace our route along the green road, walking east. The three standing stones are now opposite us, stark against the sky at the top of the hill across the R595 road. At the gate we turn right onto the R595. Opposite is a gate, with a 'No duty of care' notice on it; the landowner kindly has not said 'No Entry' but is justifiably protecting himself against injury claims. I can give no directions and no encouragement to trespassers. Clearly, walkers do sometimes cross the field to view the Three Fingers, as the stones are called. Gorse and boggy ground intervene.

The stone row, viewed from the south, stands tall and thin on the hill's saddle against a near and far landscape of bog, pine plantation, rough land and mountain. Unfortunately, a large house, perhaps a mile away, is dead centre in the view. When we think of standing stones, we think of robust items the height of cow scratching posts in a pasture. These are more like 'pillar' stones, or even drunken telegraph poles when seen from afar. On close view, they prove to be grey columns, patterned with lichen. Two are over 3.6m (12 feet) tall, with another, fallen, about the same. What a monument they are, that they should have stood for perhaps 4,000 years, aligned with the sun rising on Midsummer Day.

To reach Castletownshend village, the next attraction on our itinerary, we have no option but to use the main road. Again, caution should be exercised.

After the village name plaque, a high stone wall on the left bounds the castle estate. The small cottages, opposite, were the habitations of the Irish, situated outside the village proper, as was the Catholic church, 1.6km (1 mile) back. Castletownshend was a unique Protestant, Anglo-Irish village, an enclave of the ascendancy, with the 'wild Irish' all around.

(4) The village street, descending from the impressive gates of an estate that once included a donkey sanctuary, is immediately striking and like

no other in Ireland. Small cottages, once homes of the Irish and now painted in bright West Cork colours give way to the stolid Georgian houses built by the Anglos farther down. There are attractive oddities, 'Fuchsia', like a twee Olde English cottage, and Sundial House, with its dial over the door, tall chimney, and brick-corniced windows. The 'flower pot', as it is known, stands in mid-street, two sizeable trees growing out of it. There is a lovely Georgian house on the left and 'the billiard room' – as it once was – on the right. After Mary Ann's pub, with its various 'Good Food' recommendations, elegant townhouses line the pavements all the way down to the Townshends' Gothic pile.

(5a) The castle, built on the site of an older castle burnt down in 1856, now functions as a private residence and guest house. The grounds, well treed with some exotics, are private, and run down to the sheltered bay. A Colonel Richard Townsend received large grants of land here from the English parliament under the Act of Settlement 1652. The spelling of the name seems appropriate, considering that they did, in fact, live at the end of the town. However, this was later changed to Townshend, like the ennobled Townshends in England.

(5b) With the castle gate on the left, we take the lane down to the pier; old warehouses are being renovated as holiday homes on the right and, on the pier, the old granary has become apartments. The pier is colourful and busy in summer, with yachts and regattas. On the opposite shore is Reen Quay; farther up, a pebble shoal and the impressive ruins of Raheen, an O'Donovan castle.

A boat slip runs down onto a pebble beach and, on the rocks, acorn barnacles thrive by the million, small miracles of nature often unnoticed. Many seaweeds cover these and local rocks, each with its special zone between low and high water, although zones overlap. Bladder wrack, at mid-tide level, has two or three air bladders arranged on each side of the midrib. Sugar kelp, long and thin, with frilly edges is often found washed up here. When dried, the fronds have a white 'icing sugar' deposit, much enjoyed in China and Japan. Amateur weather forecasters use it to gauge humidity.

On the way back up to the village, we pass a fine house which apparently belongs to a dog – 'Prince's House', the sign says, with a portrait of the owner, a collie.

(5c) Again passing the castle gates, we turn right up a cloister-like lane, with the Townshend walls on our right, hung with red, or 'spur' valerian from May onwards, a lovely garden escape now common on old town walls, even in Cork city. A sign announces St Barrahane's Church of Ireland church, with a fine hexagonal stone tower just ahead. Glen Barrahane was the old name for this whole valley, called after a native saint. It was later called and written 'Castlehaven' by the English and finally was named after its most important family. One often hears West Cork people refer to Castletownshend as Castlehaven.

Wide steps climb to the church, with an iron arch overhead and a yew tree on each side. Headstones of parishoners stand randomly about the well-kept grounds, shaded by Scots pine and Ti palms, and bright with orange montbretia and the spiked white flowers of New Zealand liberti in summer.

It is a lovely church, with a patina of time and an ambience of solid sanctity and patriotism (to Britain, of course). A huge, rather vainglorious, marble tablet in a nave commemorates the history of the Townshend family while, in the church proper, more famous than any of Castletownshend's famous sons, her famous daughters, Edith Somerville and her cousin and collaborator, Violet Florence Martin (Martin Ross), authors of Some Experiences of an Irish RM (1899), are remembered in a plaque erected by American admirers. Their simple graves lie side by side behind the church, two Irish yews over them, the sea below.

The ambient light in the church has an ecclesiastical glow, filtered through stained glass windows, reflecting on dark tiled floors and polished benches. Three of the windows are by Harry Clarke (1899 to 1931), premier stained glass artist of his time, reflecting the art nouveau influence of Beardsley and Arthur Rackham. One depicts St Patrick and St George looking at one another across the Irish Sea.

(6) The village is a cul-de-sac; to leave it we must return the way we came, uphill and sharp right, past the walls of the Somerville's Drishane House on the left and taking the left turning, signed 'Tragumna 10km'. The 'coast road', as it is called, is well treed, the ditches resplendent with primroses in April, flag iris – the French fleur-de-lys – in May, foxgloves in June, navelwort in July, montbretia in August, sometimes – due to microclimates and Gulf Stream vagaries – the whole lot blooming at once. We pass a roadside well at a house entrance, on the

Inside the walls of Knockdrum Fort   *Tracarta*

right. Soon, we have close views of Horse Island. Prehistory is in the fields all about us, a ring fort to the right, cromlechs, standing stones and cup-marked stones on the left.

(7) At the T-junction, we take a sharp left down to Castlehaven Castle, the most of 1.6km (1 mile) there and back, but worth the walk. The road goes very steeply down, with dramatic views of the islands, to an apron of concrete above the pebble beach. In front, the sea; behind, an ancient graveyard and Glenbarahane Church, already in ruins in 1615 – the parish church had become St Barahane's in Castletownshend. Beyond it, on the shore, is a holy well. The church is reduced to a single gable; inside it, fuchsia grows luxuriantly within the railings of an old tomb. The headstones are mainly stumps of weathered rock, with a few memorials as late as the 1970s, one even blanketed in artificial flowers. Snowdrops bloom here in January, once, no doubt, planted, now growing wild.

(8) As we look out to sea, the ruins of Castlehaven Castle which, literally, collapsed in 1924, are on the 'cliff' at the bottom of the hill on our right. The stones are barely detectable, ivy covered and low. Dean Swift stayed there on a visit from Dublin in 1735. Once it was as grand as Raheen Castle, the O'Donovan tower house opposite Castletownshend; now it might be the ruins of a peasant *bothán*.

On the way back up the glen to the main road, birdwatchers might look out for sparrowhawks. At the main road, we turn left, continuing west as we were before we diverted.

(9) At Castlehaven Cross Roads, the footsore may take the road turning right, over the hill for a shorter way home. (The more energetic may choose to go left, walking south around the 'square' which provides a circuit of Tracarta Strand and Sandy Cove – see * below.) The road turning right climbs steadily to about 120m, with fine views to the north and to Flea and Horse Islands, south. Prehistory is, again, close by (a ring fort to the right), and modern, somewhat tragic, history, a 'cillín', to the left. Here, unbaptised children were buried; also suicides and the unidentified dead.

(10) and (11) We bear right at the two Y-junctions we meet. The ditches on either side support a host of maidenhair ferns, hard ferns, hart's-tongue, polypody, wall rue, club moss and lichens. Shortly, Knockdrum can been seen atop the hill, and we are back where we started, on the R596, in front of the school.

* The circuit to Tracarta Strand and Sandy Cove

As we walk towards the sea, the high cliffs before Scullane Point are across the water to our right and, ahead, Horse Island, with a round tower erected to mark Castlehaven Harbour. A side road left leads down to Tracarta Strand, a pebble beach, with two idyllic houses, with many flowers. Blue lesser periwinkle is in bloom in January, and lily, forget-me-not and montbretia have rooted almost on the sand. There are black-and-white oystercatchers, with red bills, out on the rocks, and many gulls.

From Tracarta, we return to the road and, walking west, enjoy wonderful views over the big bay between us and Scullane, white water beating the black cliffs in winter, mirror-calm and painted red by the sun setting on a summer evening. At the sharp corner, Sandy Cove, a small white beach, lies below us, reached by many steps.

We walk north from the cove and, at Sandycove Cross Roads, turn right. The road is largely straight, and pleasant, with much fuchsia in the hedges and little traffic. We shortly arrive back at Castlehaven Cross Roads, where we turn left up the hill on the shorter route home mentioned in (9) above.

The lake below Knockdrum Fort

CAPE CLEAR ISLAND WALK

> **Key points:** Pagan pillar stone and Christian shrine – old signal tower and lighthouse – the harbour and Bird Observatory – the Fort of Gold

Start/finish: North Harbour, Cape Clear Island, grid ref.: V955218

Distance: 6.5km (4 miles)
Map: OSi Sheet 88 **Walking time:** 3 to 4 hours

Cape Clear Island, *Oileán Chléire,* in Roaringwater Bay is 5km (3 miles) long and 3 km (2 miles) wide. Ferries make the 10km (6 mile) crossing from Baltimore in approximately forty-five minutes. The island is a Gaeltacht, a thriving community speaking Irish and English with equal ease. The population, numbering 110, includes fishermen, farmers, artists and craftsmen, with holidaymakers arriving in summer. North Harbour, where the ferries arrive, is the hub. Beyond, the boreens are as empty and unspoiled as any walker would wish for.

(1) We start our outing with an exploration of the North Harbour, where the ferries come in, a colourful scene with brightly painted boats at anchor in the docks, and the relics of history all around us. Over centuries, *Trá Chiaráin* ('St Ciarán's Strand'), as it is called, has seen the comings and goings of the islanders and their enterprises. An earlier name was *Fionn Tráigh Cléire* ('the Fair Strand of Cléire') and this may have given the island its name: 'clerus' possibly referred to 'clerk' or 'clergy', evidence of the island's ancient association with Christianity. St Ciarán was born on *Cléire* in AD 352. Patrick did not arrive in Ireland until 432 and, according to an old island saying, Patrick never came west of Leap (near Skibbereen), because the western people had already been Christianised by Ciarán and his brother Céim.

As we look out to sea, the ruined twelfth-century church of *Cill Chiarán* is to the left, possibly built on an ancient chapel raised by the saint himself. Behind the strand, near the Marian shrine, is a pillar stone,

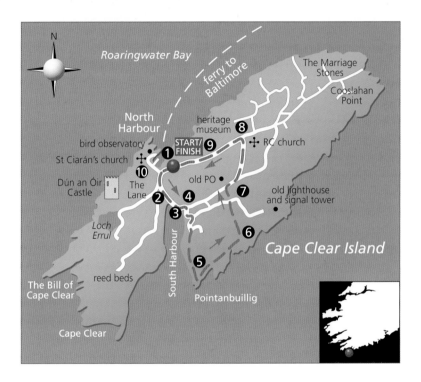

probably pre-Christian and indicating that the site was always sacred; crosses are carved into it, the stamp of the new faith. There is, also, a holy well, where pilgrims come to take water on Ciarán's Day, 5 March.

Farther to the left of the strand is the Bird Observatory, venue of twitchers from all over the world. It was Ireland's first observatory, founded in 1959. Cape Clear, so far to the south, is often the first landfall for exhausted migrants. Rare avian vagrants regularly show up here, as do rare human ones in pursuit of 'ticks' and sightings.

Leaving the harbour, we pass the shop-cafe and walk uphill, keeping right; we ignore the steep road going left to the church. After

The ferry, the Cailín Óir in North Harbour | The Marian shrine with pagan bullaun stone in front, North Harbour

passing the memorial to those drowned in the Fastnet Yacht Race in 1979, we pass a pub, then a quaint old postbox and an old stone house with quarry slates on the roof. A road goes right, signposted 'Loch Ioral'; we ignore this – we can walk it later if we wish.

(2) We go left, passing a house with distinctive bollards in front, then various houses, a pub and cottages. In August, the roadside and fields are splashed with the vivid orange of flowering montbretia. Hybridised in France as a garden exotic, it escaped from flower beds and, in Ireland, has added colour to the wild landscape. On Cape Clear, it is still in bloom in November. We pass a grotto, and a plaque to St Ciarán.

Now sheltered South Harbour is ahead, with steep land rising on the other side. A seat and a pay-as-you-view telescope overlook it and Thrush Glen, also called The Nordy Wood. The boggy ground supports goat willow, flag iris and spike rush. Heather, Irish dwarf gorse, bracken and montbretia colonise the white quartzite-type rock on the roadside cuttings.

The water in the harbour below is very blue and clear when the sun is shining. At the time of writing, three yurts stand above the shore. Available for rent, they are, I'm told, extremely warm and comfortable, indeed luxurious, with wooden beds and floors, carpets, cushions and wood-burning stoves. These, and a Native-American-style tepee, add an exotic, if somewhat incongruous, feature to the camping ground on the wild slope on the western side of South Harbour. Farther towards the western tip is the ruin of a 'fish pallace'. Many such 'pallaces' were built along the West Cork coast. As far back as the fifteenth century, pilchards arrived in their millions each summer and were harvested by locals and boats from Britain, France and Spain. In the pallaces, 'train oil', for lamps and for tanning leather, was extracted from the fish, using large presses. Later, when the shoals of pilchard mysteriously disappeared, vast harvests of mackerel and herring replaced them.

We pass what was once the priest's house, fronted by the Millennium Wall with a limestone plaque engraved 'Cléire 2000'. We ignore a turning to the left, going uphill to the National School. Next, we pass the youth hostel. There is a picnic table beside the pebbly beach, called *Trá Mór*; it is a pleasant place to pause and take in the scene.

(3) Just before the old Telegraph Station, set up in the 1860s, we go left (the route is waymarked) on the road to the old lighthouse. The Telegraph Station fulfilled a unique and, indeed, historic role. As liners from the US passed, a boat would be rowed out to collect sealed containers thrown overboard with the latest news from America; this would then be cabled forward, ahead of the liner's arrival in the UK. Thus, the humble people of *Oileán Chléire* were the first Europeans to know of the American Civil War and the assassination of Abraham Lincoln.

(4) We walk uphill rounding a bend or two before a waymark for The Glen Loop directs us into a surfaced driveway leading to a white house. Before we reach it, a sign saying 'Hikers' and a second waymark directs us through a gap in the ditch onto a narrow path. We follow this foot-worn route in single file out onto the headland of Pointanbuillig. We are walking through low-growing Irish gorse and heather, resplendent in early autumn but in springtime not yet in bloom. Here and there are stands of the taller French gorse, which may flower at any time of the year, although April and May are the best months. The views become

increasingly spectacular, our surroundings increasingly wild. This is a route to compare with any in Ireland for wildness and beauty and, because we are on an island, all the more unique.

Far below are the outer reaches of South Harbour, at the western tip of which is a slope of bare rock with what appears, at first, to be an aperture at its centre, like the eye of a needle. In fact, it is called The Eye and fishermen had a traditional rule – no doubt born of experience – that if no fish was caught between *Trá Mór* and The Eye, they might as well ship their tackle and turn their boats towards home. We may well see gannets quartering the waters of the harbour below us.

Along the pathway in springtime, we will see primroses, violets, and sun spurge; also, viviparous lizards, Ireland's only reptile.

(5) From the headland, there are magnificent views out over the Atlantic, 'the western ocean' as the Blasket Islanders called it. The Fastnet Rock with its lighthouse is the only permanent feature; it stands silhouetted against the sea. It is a lonely station, manned from when it was built in 1904 until 1989. Its light is 48.5m (159ft) above the sea. Yet, as one former Fastnet keeper put it, in stormy winter weather, the 'big seas would come sailing up over the entire building like the field of horses in the Grand National'.

From the dizzy height of the Pointanbuillig, we look down on cliffs and rock platforms. As we move along, we can see a wave-worn arch through the bare outcrop that forms the tail of the headland. Fulmar, small seagulls with beaks like miniature Derringer pistols, one barrel above the other, drift on stiff, outstretched wings below us. Guillemots and razorbills may be seen, black spots on the sea, hunting in parties; they, along with fulmar, gulls, shags and cormorants, nest all along the cliffs below.

Looking west, the white structures at Crookhaven Sheemon Point Lighthouse, at the entrance to Crookhaven on the mainland, can be seen with binoculars. Directly north is Mount Gabriel, rising behind Schull; one may see the golf-ball-like domes of the tracking station on the summit.

We encounter a stone wall here and there. A Cork University study of Irish field-wall building noted that walls on Cape Clear displayed particular characteristics depending upon their location on the island. From this, the researchers discovered that individual families traditionally built their stone walls in different patterns.

We are heading northeast along the cliff tops. We see, ahead, the signal tower and the old lighthouse. Signal towers were built along the southwest coast in 1804, following English nervousness after the French invasion attempts at Bantry Bay in 1796 and Killala Bay in 1798. Each tower was within view of two others, to ring the coast with an early-warning system. A signal fire lit on one would alert those nearest, and thus along the chain.

The lighthouse, built of granite shipped from Cornwall, was in use until 1854. However, located almost 152m (500 ft) above the sea, it was often blanketed in fog or low cloud and many an ill-fated mariner, rounding the Mizen, stayed too close to shore, leading to shipwreck on the Calf Islands, Cape Clear itself or Sherkin. When the *Stephen Whitney*, an American liner, foundered on the West Calf with the loss of ninety lives in 1847, the outcry led to the building of the first Fastnet Lighthouse in 1854, and the decommissioning of the Clear Island light.

(6) We take the waymarked path downhill before we reach the signal tower to join the tarred road below.

Our route along South Harbour takes us to the roads in the foreground

Old lighthouse and Napoleonic signal tower

(7) Upon reaching it, we turn right and follow it briefly to a waymarked stone stile on the left. This stile is also marked by a sign on the telegraph post on the right of the road, opposite it. Now, we follow a well-defined trail (a traditional Mass Path, leading to the church). We pass through low woodland (in the copses to our left, the Bird Observatory suspends its mist-nets to trap and ring migrant birds). Now, the path takes us along the boundaries of the Goat Farm. When goats are grazing in the fields, the electric fence on our left is live and should be avoided.

Leaving the goat farm behind us, we reach the crest of the hill and panoramic views open up over the Roaringwater Bay islands to the mainland and Mount Gabriel with, beyond it too low to see, Dunmanus Bay, then The Sheep's Head (Muntervary) and Hungry Hill on distant Beara Peninsula. The nearest islands are the three Calf Islands. North of them lies Long Island with Schull town to the right, Heir Island to the northeast and, between it and the mainland, Castle and Horse islands.

(8) The Mass Path emerges at the church, where we turn left. The church was built in 1839 on the site of an older church, which had a thatched roof and was said to be 'as destitute of ornament as any barn'. The present church is also a plain and unfussy place of worship, with an aura of sanctity and peace. *Cosán an tSléibhe*, the path that crosses the island, emerges in a neat stile by the western gable.

Beyond the church is the Heritage Centre, until 1897 a National School for girls. It houses many items of interest in the long history of *Oileán Chléire*, with a collection of 1,500 photographs by Michael Minihane of the *Irish Examiner,* Pierce Hickey and other photographers. It is open daily through June, July and August, and otherwise a key is available at the library or on the island bus. Various artefacts, including a quern stone for grinding grain, are exhibited outside.

(9) On the right, is Cléire Goat Farm, where one may stop to enjoy a goat's milk ice cream or yoghurt. The owner, who is blind, is English and has been resident on the island for many years. He is a great singer of ballads. Wayside plaques tell us about the lighthouse, off to the south and, once again, we have magnificent views of the Fastnet Light on the horizon, 6.5km (4 miles) away, and of the whole western end of the island, with a ruined castle midway along the northwest shore.

This is *Dún an Óir*, 'The Fort of Gold', one of the last castles left to Fineen O Driscoll, 'the Rover' (see Sherkin Island Walk).

This is a lovely route downhill. The field walls are made of stones cleared from the land, thus fulfilling two purposes. Expansive vistas open before us. We can see both sides of the island and we have a bird's-eye view of the little port below. St Ciarán is said to have been born near here in AD 352; his birth is recorded in the *Annals of Innisfallen*, written in the eleventh century at an island monastery in Lough Leane, in Killarney.

We soon reach the junction, with the harbour, our starting point, below us on our right.

(10) Should we have the energy, and it is evening and fair weather, we might walk a little beyond the ruined St Ciarán's church and the graveyard, and come on distant and romantic views of *Dún an Óir* castle perched on the cliffs. As the sun sets over the broad Atlantic and its last rays touch the walls, we can indeed see why it was called 'The Fort of Gold'.

Views of the 'western ocean' from the path, Cape Clear

SHERKIN ISLAND WALK

> **Key points:** Sherkin Friary – O'Driscoll castle – The Dock – inshore marine flora and fauna – white sand beaches – famous Marine Station

Start/finish: the pier on the east end of the island, where the ferry arrives, grid ref.: W028257

Distance: 14.5km (9 miles)
Map: OSi Sheet 88 **Walking time:** 3 to 4 hours

The old name for Sherkin is *Inis Archáin*, 'Archain's Island'. This may come from orca, the killer whale, as in the case of Orkney, off the Scottish coast, or it may mean the island of sea-pigs or porpoises; *arcáin* was the Irish word for these. Others believe it derives from the name Ciarán as in St Ciarán of nearby Cape Clear Island. The source is uncertain, indeed 'arcane'.

The island is some 5km (3 miles) long and 2km (1.2 miles) wide, with a resident population of about 100. The land is good, but for the south shore and the slopes of Slievemore, and there are pleasant bathing beaches. The ferry takes fifteen minutes from Baltimore (see ferry and cable-car timetables). A seal often surfaces in the Baltimore dock, watching the people come and go.

(1) A steep road leads up from the pier, past the ruined friary. Overnight visitors set off carrying their luggage; recently, a rural bus and a taxi service has been established, but nowhere is very far and many visitors opt to walk.

At the time of writing, conservation work on the friary is ongoing. The work began in 1986, and the bell tower has since been repaired, with new oak floors and oak roof timbers. A Franciscan house founded by the O'Driscolls in about 1460, it was burnt in 1537 by Waterford raiders, smarting from the expropriation of 18,000 gallons of wine by Fineen O'Driscoll from a Waterford-bound ship that sheltered in

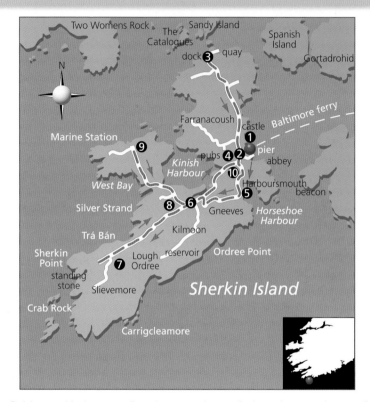

Baltimore Harbour earlier that year. In retaliation, the merchants of Waterford sent a force of 400 men, led by an English adventurer. They 'invaded' Sherkin, seized the castle, and spent five days ravaging the island, burning the villages, abbey and castle, and scuttling or seizing the O'Driscoll fleet. The castle was rebuilt, but was taken by Spaniards in 1602, after the final Irish defeat at Kinsale the previous year. Sir Fineen accommodated them, supplying artillery and ammunition. When the English seized it, Sir Fineen, who had played both sides, was lucky to lose only his lands and not his life. Once lord of many castles and the islands of Roaringwater Bay, he died destitute in his last remaining tower house at Lough Hyne.

Sherkin Friary

The plants on the earth-and-stone wall on our left as we walk towards the telephone box are worth notice. Here, amongst others, may be found Sherkin's only crop of Bird's Foot, a rare small white flower of early March. There is also heath speedwell, germander speedwell, stonecrop, and various ferns. Sherkin has the largest flora of all the islands of the bay, the most trees and the best-developed scrubland.

On the leylandii above the road on the right, opposite the abbey, one sees the effect of the prevailing winds. As we reach the junction, we take the road going right signposted for the Islander's Rest hotel and the Jolly Roger pub. Birds are in profusion, all the familiar species, and grey crows (hooded crows) which may not be familiar to visitors from the UK.

(2) Just beyond the Islander's Rest, a right turn takes us down to the remains of Dunalong ('the Fort of the Ships'), an O'Driscoll castle, now a stumpy, ivy-covered tower. Wild parsley, growing on the walls, and black mustard, with its yellow flowers, are perhaps survivors of an ancient kitchen garden.

Back on the tarmac, the road winds gently north between high ditches colonised by hart's-tongue ferns, French gorse, primroses, foxgloves, yarrow and a host of other wild plants, each flowering in its season. There are wide views across the water to Ringarogy and Spanish Island. In spring and summer, the background sounds are bird-song and the humming of bees; it is worth watching for unusual birds, as rare migrants sometimes make a landfall here.

The sea below us is often calm, with the rocks jet black against the brilliant ultramarine. Shabby-looking cormorants stand silhouetted on the shore, hanging out their wings to dry. New houses are going up here and there, but Sherkin remains part of 'the peaceful kingdom' of nature.

Topping a small rise, we see rocks and islands laid out before us, Heir Island and its pier, the pier at Cunnamore, Sandy Island and The Catalogues. From late March, these are ablaze with gorse; beyond them are channels of bright water, blue hills and the bulk of Mount Gabriel where, nearly 4,000 years ago, the pre-Celtic Irish mined copper before any other Europeans and, mixing it with tin from Cornwall, made bronze. Now, huge, white 'golf balls', monitoring North Atlantic air and sea traffic, top the summit.

(3) The road leads down to a small pier called The Dock with various boats in states of repair or disrepair and stacked lobster pots. Here, there was once a boatbuilding industry. Nearby, a wide beach is exposed at low tide, and one can walk to the offshore islets. Small

Dunalong, on Sherkin

Horseshoe Harbour, Sherkin

The Dock, Sherkin

mullet cruise in the shallows and the cove is a delight for the amateur marine biologist or the child with a shrimping net. *A Beginner's Guide to Ireland's Seashore*, published by Sherkin Island Marine Station, is invaluable. For the expert, Gillian Bishop's *Ecology of the Rocky Shores of Sherkin Island*, also published by the Marine Station, provides a wealth of data.

Low water provides a chance to see most of the common seaweeds, each having its own niche and specific zone, nearer or farther from the tide mark. About 3m (10ft) up the rock walls on the left, channelled wrack survives in the high-water splash zone; moisture held in the channels on the fronds keeps it alive, unsubmerged, for days. At the base of the rocks, sugar kelp, like flattened barley sugar, and oarweed, a kelp with a strong stipe or stem, is submerged at all but the lowest tides. Nearby, almost the entire inshore flora may be found, including sea lettuce, laver and edible carrageen.

In summer, there are small fish, shannies and gobies, in the rock pools, and crabs and prawns. Clinging to the sides are liver-red beadlet anemones with brilliant blue 'beads' around the 'neck' from which the tentacles emerge; they tickle your fingers 'electrically' if you touch them. Millions of tiny, white acorn barnacles cling to the rocks, along with limpets, shaped like cones, periwinkles, with black, snail-like shells, and white dog whelks, with a groove at the shell mouth allowing a small 'snorkel' to be raised as they crawl over mud. They have a drill-like tongue and bore through the shells of mussels to suck out the soft body inside. We find shells on the beach with neat holes drilled in them.

On the beach, sand masons, exotic marine worms, put up tubes of sand, fringed with a sandy mop-head to protect the delicate tentacles which they raise to filter food when the tide covers them. The spaghetti-like whorls of lugworms are everywhere, with holes close by; the worm is 13cm (1ft) beneath the sand, roughly between the two.

Rocks above the tide line are colonised with white flowering scurvy grass, sea pinks, and lichens, especially grey-green Neptune's Beard (sea ivory) and orange *Xanathoria*.

We return to the friary corner the way we came. En route, we may notice items of interest that were hidden on the outward leg.

(4) and (5) At the corner, we turn right, passing a framed map of the island, and go left at the phone box, taking the sign for Horseshoe Harbour. We are now on a track, with a gate to the left, to the lighthouse and a private residence. We pass house ruins and Horseshoe Cottage, a B&B decorated with nets and net-balls. We go through a gate and shortly have a view down to the (usually) mirror-calm waters of Horseshoe Harbour. It is clear why it is described as a 'horseshoe'; it is a perfect amphitheatre, with its mouth opening to the sea.

We cross a stile and the path narrows to a grassy track. Foxgloves hang over it in June, and bees buzz busily in the sun trap of the lane. The heather- and gorse-covered slopes and the deep blue of the harbour make this circuit idyllic in summer. A few pretty houses, accessible only on foot, look down on it. Blackthorn blooms over the water in March, whitethorn in May, montbretia in August, fuchsia into October – never a colourless day once spring arrives.

We go downhill. At the lowest point, there is a platform of soft grass over the sea. A stream crosses the path, muddy in wet weather. As it climbs the slope to Gneeves, on the south side, the path becomes a stream bed in wet weather. As we gradually ascend, the small, neat, Sherkin lighthouse and keeper's cottage come into view across the harbour. Reaching the crest, we come upon a shale road into a house.

We turn right and set off downhill to join the main island road. We can see it below us. We have views of lone houses on distant headlands, and of the church, with its bell arch, beside the road, with the Atlantic and the islands beyond.

After some scrubby land, we pass a small pond, with spike rush, flag iris and willow. Kinish Harbour, like a sea lake with its narrow mouth, is now seen. There are some pines on the right. Soon afterwards, we pass the entrance to a small estate of relatively new local authority houses; there are other houses, also, nearby.

(6) We come out opposite a sheltered lagoon, cut off from Kinish by a low wall, covered at high tide. We turn left. Sycamores and alders arch over the road ahead and we pass through a dappled, leafy tunnel. This is a sheltered spot, with attractive houses and gardens half hidden behind escalonia hedges. In August, the verges beyond the 'tunnel' are bright with the brilliant orange of montbretia in flower. We ignore the road to the right, and continue southwest, towards *Trá Bán*.

We reach the church, with its three arched windows and bell arch above the gable. The crown of the macrocarpa tree, in front of the house alongside, is planed flat by the wind. Now, on the roadside stone walls, lichens thrive, notably crispy lungwort and sea ivory.

The road is straight and traffic-free. Behind Schull, to the northwest, Mount Gabriel looms large against the sky; nearer true north, in the middle distance, a castle stands lonely on the mainland shore. Cape Clear Island comes into view ahead, with its signal tower. *Trá Bán*, the 'white strand', a horseshoe-shaped sandy beach, is below us on the right. The islands to the north are Heir Island, the three Calf Islands, and beyond, Castle and Long Islands, west of Schull.

(7) The road divides in a Y. We follow the right 'arm', a grassy track, past an old stone house and down towards the sea. Black rocks lie between us and Clear Island, which rises very high, with the signal tower and some houses silhouetted against the sky.

We turn and retrace our steps. Now as we walk east towards the church, we see, in the middle distance, the sweep of West Bay to the north, with its two sandy beaches. The long, low buildings beyond the second beach are part of the Marine Station, housing libraries and high tech labs, reached by tracks across unshorn fields.

(8) After passing the church, we take the road to the left, signposted Silver Strand. Stands of large sycamores and witch hazels edge the road. We shortly arrive at an 'isthmus', with Kinish Harbour on our right, a pebbly shore. Now a path across some small dunes, held together with marram, leads onto Silver Strand.

(9) Continuing, we pass a road to the left which leads to the Marine Station and an ancient promontory fort. The road straight ahead takes us to close views of Heir Island. There is no 'loop' route, so we must now retrace our steps to the main road, where we turn left, heading for the pier and the ferry. The route back takes us, again, along the Kinish lagoon. Little egrets, a relatively new bird in Ireland, may be seen here, stalking the shallows. There is a spinney of holly and Scots pine in a field on our right. We pass the new school, in modern prefab buildings, in front of the old schoolhouse, neatly painted and well maintained. 'Sherkin Male National School, 1892', says a plaque on the front wall and, at the rear, another plaque announces, 'Sherkin Island Girls' and Boys' National School 1892 – 1992'.

A house on a promontory over Kinish has a large yacht drawn up beside the garden; the harbour must be deep at high tides. We pass the Community Centre, and the library. As we head along the road towards the ferry, below, on the left, we may see the ripples of the fat, slow mullet which come into Rugher Strand with each tide.

(10) Topping the rise, we walk downhill towards the abbey and the pier. Sometimes, in summer, the bay is full of mackerel as we cross, with white terns screaming and, farther out, big, white, cruciform gannets, with black wing tips, diving on the shoals.

Silver Strand

RINGAROGY ISLAND

Key points: a gentler pace — country lanes — few cars, much nature

Start/finish: the east end of Lag Bridge, off the Skibbereen–Baltimore R595 road, grid ref. W059292.

Distance: 6.5km (4 miles)
Map: OSi Sheet 88 **Walking Time:** 1 hour 30 minutes

Ringarogy means 'point of the small portion'. This, perhaps, refers to the island, an O'Driscoll estate, as a small holding compared to their extensive mainland demesnes. In Ringarogy, the peace and quiet of another era still obtains. The houses may be modern or modernised but the roads are lanes and one rarely sees a car. There are few human artefacts to distract us from nature. The stones of the O'Driscoll castle that once stood at the north end were spirited off to build the cathedral at Skibbereen in 1826. A small *cillín* and perhaps a dozen houses are passed on the entire 6.5km (4-mile) route. Once, almost 800 people lived here; now, there are about 70. I can think of few more pleasant walks in West Cork.

(1) We set off at the west side of the causeway known as the Lag Bridge. The River Ilen washes the northwest shore of Ringarogy. Here, on the southeast side, the Lag is a silted-up channel, filled and emptied by the tides, a 'lag' or area of low ground between mainland and island.

If the tide is out and it is winter, one is immediately arrested by the bird life. Out on the mudflats between the small islets and rocks, a dozen species stalk or waddle about, identifiable with the naked eye. If it is summer, there will be far fewer, but there will be some. If the tide is in, one should look out for birds on the shores; they will not be as easy to see but some colourful species – e.g. black-and-white oystercatchers, with bright red bills – will be obvious, and others will be roosting near them.

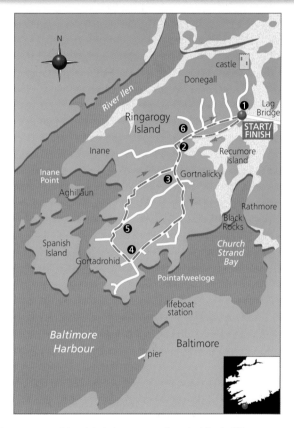

The most striking birds here are the shelduck. They are present all year but are fewer in July and August when most adults fly to Heligoland, in the Baltic, or to the Bristol Channel. The shelduck do, in fact, eat shells – the tiny hydrobia snails which they hoover by the thousand off the mud flats have thin, whorled shells – but they are not called for that, rather for the old word 'sheld' meaning variegated and referring to their colour.

Out on the slob, redshank, greenshank, curlew and oystercatchers stalk insects and worms; a cubic metre of estuary mud is said to contain more life than a cubic metre of Amazon top soil. The redshank's call will be one of the first sounds heard, clear, fluting notes – *tu-ee, tu-ee, tu-ee* – redolent of wildness and loneliness. Ever wary, it rises as we pass, a thin, brown wader, known in flight by its white wing edges, white rump and tail, and red legs trailing. It bobs and ducks as it struts about the shallows, much more nervous that its cousin, the greenshank (green legs, taller and whiter, and a white V up its back as it flies) which is generally seen alone. Some 500 greenshank cross from Scotland to Ireland in winter, while redshank, including Iceland immigrants, may number 25,000. About 5,000 redshank breed here, on lake shores and in the Shannon callows.

Sheltered waters, Ringarogy

Channelled wrack, a short seaweed, thrives on the rocks along the edge of the causeway. It forms a distinct belt, defining the upper level of the tides. It has no 'bubbles' but can hold water in the 'channels' of the fronds and so avoid desiccation when tide levels fall for a few days.

We walk southwest. Gorse and heather skirt the lane; the trees we will encounter, apart from a few pines, are sallies, goat willow and alder. The sally bushes bear furry buds in spring; the alders have catkins and small cones. The gorse is French Gorse, spring flowering and up to 1.8m (6ft) high, and dwarf gorse which flowers in autumn, with the heather. Gorse seeds from Ireland were taken to Scotland and Wales to grow fodder for cattle. The islets and islands of the Lag and the bay are dressed twice a year in mantles of yellow, or yellow and purple. The shoreline rocks are splattered with white and orange lichens. The rocks are black, the sheltered waters dark, reflecting all these colours.

As we hoof it along the road, away to the southeast is the signal tower behind Baltimore and, nearby, we have new views of the slob, with silver or blue channels running between the mud, depending on the colour of the sky. Other ducks, red-headed widgeon from Iceland, Scandinavia, Russia and Siberia, and tiny teal, some Irish, some Continental, frequent these secluded places.

Sedge edges the road for a few yards; streams inside and outside the road ditch are regular, with spike rush, amphibious bistort and fools watercress thriving. A road merges from the right – we will be returning to the causeway along it. This area is Donegall West; the old name for the island is Dunnegal. There are rhododendron clumps here and there. It has either been culled here or has some natural restriction; it is an extremely invasive species in areas of high rainfall and acid soils, swallowing up huge tracts of land, wiping out all native, ground-dwelling flora – but it does have glorious purple blooms in early spring.

(2) We branch sharply left at a corner, taking the wider road and ignoring the road straight ahead (which goes to a townland spelt Inane but pronounced, no doubt, In-ahn). Here, there is much honeysuckle on the ditch beneath a brake of alders. Typically, the alders grow by a stream. A bit of quarry breaks the ground on the left, with spoil heaps covered with vegetation. On the right, we have examples of 'rivers

Grey heron, Ringarogy

of green', narrow fields running down to the road between rock and gorse-grown outcrops.

Around isolated houses are wind-sculpted trees. Turning to look back, we enjoy great views over the slobs and channels of the Lag.

(3) The road divides in a Y. We do not go straight ahead but veer sharply left, rounding a corner climbing gently uphill. Shortly, there is a narrow road right; this makes a rough diagonal crossing the circle we will walk. We ignore it. There are some fuchsia hedges from here on and, on the roadside, blackthorn and whitethorn *sceacs*, their branches permed like windblown hair. As the road descends gently, we see Spanish Island and the mouth of the Ilen to the right, Turk Head and, far off, Mount Gabriel, behind Schull. There is a small pond on our left, full only in winter. Soon, Baltimore is seen, with a line of holiday cottages below the O'Driscoll 'castle'. A fine farmhouse with a new roof is up a lane to the left and, beyond it, on the right, some stone outbuildings. Montbretia edges both sides of the road, flaming orange in August, appropriately wild-looking in this location – although it is, in fact, a French nursery 'concoction', a garden escape.

We pass a fuchsia hedge and some escalonia – both stoutly withstand salt breezes – and, below some trees on the left, a house with attractive and unusual windows, and a turquoise roof on the porch. We soon find ourselves walking downhill, with the sea straight ahead. The vicious black rocks below the Sherkin lighthouse, the white beacon on the Baltimore side and, then, the coloured houses of Baltimore come into view. The vista is large from here; Sherkin, the pier and the hinterland, Spanish Island and others.

Ringarogy, while naturally welcoming, has the most 'No trespassing' and 'The owner excludes the duty of care' notices per mile of road I have ever seen. In fact, the Occupiers' Liability Act 1995 (Section 5) protects farmers from injury or damages claims by entrants to their land and it is now, rightly, almost impossible for such claims to succeed. The walker is expected to exercise judgement. Farmers cannot be held responsible for the actions of fools – to have a bull in a field does not constitute 'reckless disregard' for those who might decide to enter it. As we know, we should avoid livestock and crops, close gates, and leave nothing behind us and take nothing with us when we leave.

(4) As we face Baltimore town, just before a ruin on the left, we swing sharp right, almost a hairpin. On the right of the road is a long line of alders, overhanging a robust little stream inside the ditch. They are spaced as if planted but this would be unusual – alders seed themselves along watercourses all over Europe, having small cones which float (they are the only deciduous cone-bearing tree). Alders thrive on wet land, fixing nitrogen with their roots, and improving it. The stand we are passing would keep a flock of siskins from October to March as the seeds slowly ripen; they take only the ripest and move from tree to tree, calling shrilly as they go.

Looking towards Baltimore from the Log Bridge

Mosses and a beautiful crinkly grey lichen, tree lungwort, flourish on these mature trees. Lichens are not one plant but a combination of organisms. Some lichens are edible, some contain antibiotics and some live for 10,000 years. Opposite, the stone wall is colonised with delicate maidenhair fern and also stout, spectacular foxgloves, over 1m (4ft) tall in a good year, covered in purple bells and a favourite of bumblebees. Honeysuckle also blooms profusely along this sheltered road.

We see the water again, ahead of us, and Mount Gabriel, far off. A perfect 'river of green' flows down to the road, with electricity poles marching up it. Two gables of a ruin stand starkly on a low hill to the west. Spanish Island is beyond – it can be reached at low tide – and, then, the sheltered inlet between us and the mouth of the Ilen.

(5) We ignore the road to the right, the south end of the 'diagonal'. The sea is now hidden by rising ground. There are big mussel shells on the road, dropped by grey crows from aloft and, once cracked, prised open.

We pass a 'dream cottage' on a trimmed green lawn by the sea and now, there is wet ground on the left, with many bright flag irises blooming in June, Irish spurge and wispy, creamy, meadowsweet in August. Meadowsweet was once strewn on the earthen floors of farmhouses for its scent, and was the first source of aspirin, the world's most widely used drug, in 1853.

We arrive back at the full round of the circle, retrace our steps

Shelduck, often seen near the Lag Bridge

Ringarogy islets, with Napoleonic signal tower above Baltimore

past the small quarry, and turn right at the T-junction (2). We pass the rhododendron, and a road to the left, and then the road splits.

(6) We take the 'high' road, the left branch of the narrow 'Y'. We pass an old farmhouse, and modern houses in pastel colours, a house with boats on the lawn and, then 'Reengaroga National School 1913' now converted to a fine dwelling house with dormer windows. This high road is a lovely walk on a summer evening when the western sun picks out the gold-and-purple of Recumore Island and the islets of the Lag, like jewels set in silver.

Just before we reach the causeway, a small brake of goat willow stands over land that is flooded in winter. Brilliant green moss clothes the trunks and branches. One late winter afternoon, when we arrived here after a shower, bright beadlets of water hung from the buds, sparkling in the sun. One poetic soul remembered the Austin Clarke line about 'brightness drenching through the branches'; and, as new waves of haze swept in across the causeway, we thought of 'the mist becoming rain'.

THE BANTRY TO DROMCLOGH LOOP OF THE SHEEP'S HEAD WAY

Key points: Bantry House and grounds – quiet country roads – cross-country, panoramic views over Bantry Bay to the Caha Mountains and beyond

Start/finish: east of Bantry town, at the gate lodge to Bantry House, grid ref.: V989484.

Distance: 5–6km, (4 miles)
Map: OSi Sheet 85 **Walking time:** 2 hours

We begin this figure-of-eight walk just east of Bantry town, on the N71, between the cinema and the Maritime Hotel, where a cut-stone gate lodge, in the form of an arch, gives access to the grounds of Bantry House. The Shelswell-White family, descendants of the Earls of Bantry, have graciously allowed walkers on the Sheep's Head Way to follow paths through these magnificent grounds. There is a waymark at the entrance. From March to October, one may also enter by the main gate, 0.5km (0.35 miles) farther along, and pick up the Sheep's Head waymarks from the car park. The notice of an entry fee relates to visiting the house interior. This is well worthwhile: Bantry House is one of the finest historic houses in Ireland.

(1) After passing through the arch, we walk up a long tree- and laurel-lined driveway with bluebells on the verges in springtime. As we near the house, a huge macrocarpa cypress catches the eye to the right, with the sea and Whiddy Island beyond and, directly west, the bulk of the Sugar Loaf Mountain on the Beara Peninsula.

(2) We reach the wrought-iron gates that lead to the visitors' entrance to Bantry House and its gardens. If we do not wish to visit either, we follow the path that curves to the left and skirts the perimeter of the gravelled car park with a circular flower bed at centre. This pathway

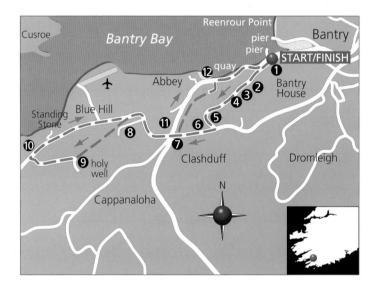

takes us past a stone building topped by a cupola, with an archway at centre leading to an enclosed yard. The path leads along the back of the house, past the parterre and fountain. In the parterre, sometimes called the Italianate gardens (the 2nd Earl emulated 'palazzo' gardens he had seen when travelling in Italy in the mid-nineteenth century), low boxwood and yew hedges are arranged in patterns, with narrow paths between. At centre is the Wisteria Circle, in full purple flower in May. At the rear of the parterre, the 'Hundred Steps' ascend to a carriage drive, from which one can enjoy panoramic views over the house and across the bay to the mountains of Beara.

While we can continue our route (by going straight ahead) a circuit of the exterior of the house is worthwhile. After passing the parterre, we notice an entrance to the Tea Rooms. Here, we can turn right at the house corner and pass a large terrace, which, with the tall, French windows behind, recalls a colonial mansion.

Rear of Bantry House

Between us and the sea, the gardens step down to flower beds and lawns. The house and grounds are, in fact, built of seven terraces, rising from the road, now the N71, which divides it from the sea.

As we turn right again to complete our circuit, the wrought-iron gates and the central garden that front the house once more come into view. We exit via the wrought-iron gates and walk again along the back of the house past the parterre.

(3) At a magnificent copper beech, the path from the main car park joins from the right. At the waymarked stone on the left of our path, we go straight ahead. A grassy meadow lies a level below us. On our left, is a wide variety of exotic trees, shrubs and plants, including gunnera and a small stand of invasive Japanese Knotweed. There are primroses, Irish spurge, lemon-yellow in springtime, and cowslips, rare in West Cork now.

(4) We reach a crossroads. The path going left rejoices in the name 'Old Ladies' Walk', although it climbs steeply and the genteel grandmammas of the Bantry Whites must have been in rude good health to tackle it. To the right, a series of flagstones leads to an exceedingly pretty 'Japanese' bridge over a small stream, with a red-leafed Japanese

maple close by. One may continue straight ahead on the waymarked gravelled path (the Woodland Walk) but a more pleasant option is to cross the bridge and follow it on a parallel, earthen path on the opposite side of the stream.

As we emerge from the earthen path, the gates of the walled garden, with its ancient apple trees and more modern vegetable patches, are on our right, with pretty filigree iron screens.

(5) We return to the gravelled path opposite the gates, where a waymark fixed to the trunk of a myrtle directs us to continue right, uphill. (There is some confusion here on the OS map: it appears that a path once led across the walled garden to the road.) We pass through a tunnel of trees. Speckled wood butterflies may be seen as early as May and as late as October. Soon, we see the backs of houses on our right and then a field gate across the path. A narrow passage between concrete posts is provided alongside it.

(6) Beyond the gate, we arrive on a road leading to the Bantry Enterprise Park, with a sign for Bantry Glass. A waymark directs us right to a road 20m (22 yards) away. Reaching the road, we may see a waymark amongst a stand of knotweed on the opposite ditch: this directs walkers left but is for those following the Sheep's Head route inland and towards Durrus. We go right, at first walking uphill.

This road is called the Rope Walk. We soon top the rise and see the bay below. An old footpath runs a metre above this wide road for a short distance – we pass houses and an impressive gate to the walled garden of Bantry House. A sign on the right for 'Kilnaurane Pillar Stone', directs us to a short lane leading to a field opposite. The site was an early ecclesiastical enclosure, with a burial ground and bullaun stone, near the summit of a hill overlooking Bantry Bay; the original structure no longer exists. As we walk downhill, the Caha Mountains on Beara rise dramatically beyond the waters of the bay.

(7) We reach the N71 and cross it to go down the small road directly opposite us, signposted Sheep's Head and Dromclogh and waymarked. A sign immediately warns motorists: 'Caution. Walkers on the road.' However, in my experience, it is a nice, quiet road. Swathes of montbretia grow along it, the orange flowers spectacular in July.

Off we go, into the country. The road undulates gently. We come

On the Bantry Walk

to a house on the right with large pines and an unusual old stone wall: perpendicular stones set in a pattern on the horizontal risers, protruding from the face.

(8) Opposite this house, on the left, is a by-road and a waymark painted on a stone low down on the ditch directing us along it. We pass between bungalows with mature gardens.

The paved lane becomes a grassy track, wide enough but, clearly, rarely used. It ends at a gate into a field. Just before it, on the right, is a waymarked field-stone stile. We cross this and walk along a grassy corridor a metre wide, with a stream on our left and a barbed-wire fence on our right. Goat willow overgrows the stream here and there, its catkins falling in the water. On the surface, a pretty plant, ivy-leaved crowfoot, may be seen in May.

At the end of the corridor is a waymarked ladder-stile, on which a crusty lichen, which I've heard called 'crottle', grows along with a 'hairy' or filamented lichen, possibly, *Ramalina siliquosa*. These ladder-stiles require some care – and effort – in negotiation.

For a short sector, rising ground to our right obscures the bay. Spear rush grows in clumps. After another stile – a tree branch is low over the apex, so care should be taken – we begin to walk uphill along cow paths. These will be slippery in winter, and one should be well shod.

The views are magnificent, especially in April and May when acres of golden gorse lie between us and the blue sea, scenting the air.

At the top of the hill (waymark no. 15) extensive stands of pines come into view below: in one, the Bantry Waste Water Treatment Plant is so well hidden that we see only a small platform with pipes and pumps above the trees. Whiddy Island, with its fine, grassy fields and, at the western end, the well-landscaped, deep-green oil storage tanks, is ever-present in this view. With binoculars, we can make out a single wall of the old fort at the eastern end of Whiddy, at the highest point, and a gull-roost on a gravel-spit protruding from the nearest shore. Binoculars give wonderful views of the stratified hills of Beara, of the Sugar Loaf and Hungry Hill, and of the mountains behind them.

West Lodge Hotel is visible due east: we will be walking past its gracious lawns later, a huge contrast to the wild fields around us and a much-appreciated off-road sector of the Sheep's Head Way. Farther east are distant hills: Mullaghmesa and Nowen Hill.

We are directed right and pass the white gate of a garden. Now, on level ground, we pass through a gap in a gorse hedge and go right across a rushy field, colonised by meadow buttercups and cuckoo flowers.

Bog myrtle

(9) We emerge onto a paved road, via a final, formidable ladder-stile. The road ends at a neat farmhouse below us on the left.

We go straight ahead, passing some older bungalows on our right and then new, larger, multi-roofed houses. The views between them, across Bantry Bay to the Caha Mountains, are breathtaking.

The road is descending now. As we get a little lower, the line of houses ends and a magnificent panorama opens below us, all the way from the western tip of Beara to Whiddy Island near the eastern end of the bay. It is a vista almost without parallel in West Cork. (Unfortunately, a huge new house below the road now dominates the very centre of the view.)

Going steeply downhill, we pass a tiny cottage. Then, also on our left, we pass corrugated iron barns rusted red, with a healthy-looking manure heap by the roadside in front. We pass houses with gardens and walk through tunnels of roadside trees. As we near the entrance to Ballyrah House on the corner of a road going sharply right, there is a waymark post on our right, but it is easy to miss in passing.

(10) We take the hairpin bend at the T-junction and go right alongside Ballyrah House entrance, with its pretty copper beech, and walk downhill on a wider road. We pass a left turn, signposted Bantry Waste Water Treatment Plant. If we wish, we can walk a few hundred metres down this road to the sea.

After retracing our steps to the Sheep's Head Way, we go left towards Bantry. Again, the road is sometimes overshadowed by trees. We pass the house with the distinctive stone wall, opposite which we earlier set out for the fields and hills. We can now see the West Lodge Hotel on the other side of the N71, ahead.

(11) Reaching the N71, we cross it and walk up the driveway of the hotel, with its shrubberies and elegant glass frontage. At the top of the driveway, a waymarked sign directs us left and we pass along the front of the building and around to the sides where there are self-catering cottages and a second car park. As we step down to the path running between the hotel lawns, the route is an extremely pretty and peaceful one. Steps on the left take us down to a paved area alongside a small pond and stream, with a picnic table, a decorative bridge and a short row of slim columns entwined with creepers. The level, green parkland stretches around us, with some fine trees.

As we walk along the path, which curves around towards the small, ornate gate lodge where our route meets the road, we have views of the bay and may see the brightly coloured Whiddy Island ferry.

(12) Beside the lodge, we pass through the open gate. We are now on the N71, facing the bay. Crossing to the pavement opposite, we walk towards the town. The visitors' entrance and car park at Bantry House are only a short distance along. If we began our walk at the entrance alongside the Maritime Hotel, we continue along the seaside footpath until we reach it. It is only a few hundred metres to the main square, with its impressive statute of St Brendan the Navigator, claimed to be the first European discoverer of America. Bantry is a lovely town and, if one has the energy, there is much of interest still to be enjoyed including the Mill Race Walk, Godson's Folly, the Union Street Steps and the Presbytery.

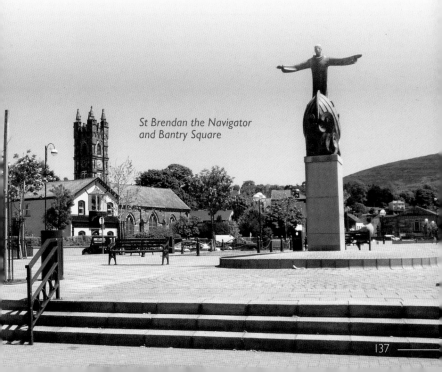

St Brendan the Navigator
and Bantry Square

THE TIP OF THE SHEEP'S HEAD

Key points: Laharandota Lough – Ballyroon Mountain – Tooreen turning point – Lough Akeen – the lighthouse

Loop A

Start/finish: Laharandota Lough, approx. 8km (5 miles) west of Kilcrohane, grid ref.: V756351

Map: OSi Sheet 88
Distance: 6.5km (4 miles) **Walking Time:** 2 hours

Loop B

Start/finish: Tooreen turning point, grid ref.: V732340

Map: OSi Sheet 88
Distance: 3.5km (2 miles) **Walking Time:** 2 hours

LOOP A

(1) We leave the car in a parking place beside Laharandota Lough and walk towards Kilcrohane, passing a smaller lough and a waymarked stile on the left. We reach an iron shed on the right, with a large rock slab bearing a *Fáilte* sign. We set off up the by-road, signposted to the signal tower.

It climbs steeply, levels and, after passing some houses, becomes a broad grass-grown track, passing another shed on the left. It is more like a turf road now and branches off to left, while we continue toward the dorsal ridge of the peninsula. A fingerpost is visible ahead; fingerposts guide us over Ballyroon Mountain to the Tooreen turning point where we can pick up the second loop or return to the lough via the road.

We pass Post 279 with rising land on both sides and the bulk of the ridge ahead of us. As we climb, the path winds through dwarf

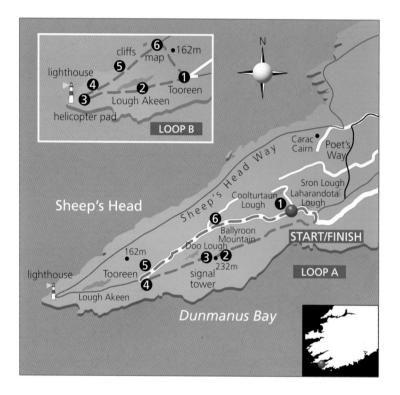

gorse and ling; occasionally, it winds between rocks and sometimes crosses a 'lag' of boggy ground. As we climb steadily higher, Bantry Bay comes into view on our right, with the Slieve Miskish Mountains on the Beara Peninsula on the other side. On clear days, we can see as far as the mountains of Iveragh, Cahernageeha and Mullaghbeg, blue and hazy in the distance. To our left is Dunmanus Bay.

(2) As we reach the signal tower, now in ruins, the hills of the Mizen Peninsula lie across the bay, Knocknamadree (313m) and, towards the tip, Knockalossonig and Mizen Peak. From here, we can see the tower

Dunmanus Bay   *A Sheep's Head ruin*

on Mizen across Dunmanus Bay and, looking north, the tower at Black Head on Beara and the tower on Dursey Island (see Dursey Island Walk).

Due south, below the tower, are the ruins of a small settlement. Leaving the tower, Lough Akeen near the tip of the peninsula comes into view.

(3) After passing the benchmark on the peak of Ballyroon (232m) and crossing a step-over stile, we arrive at a low concrete hut, a Second World War lookout post. The view is panoramic. On the north shore of Bantry Bay, we see the white cigar-shaped beacon on Bere Island and the strait between the island and Castletownbere. Doo Lough (from *an dubh loch* – the black lake) lies below us, still and dark, with reeds along the shore. We cross another stile and now, as we come down the slope towards the turning point, we see a white house below, with a pond, in a scoop of flat land.

(4) After crossing a wooden bridge and a final stile (beside it is a fingerpost with an electronic eye to count the number of walkers using the path), we arrive at the turning point and may repair to the

Sheep's Head Cafe to sample Bernie Tobin's excellent homemade fare; she can cater for large groups if informed in advance.

(5) We can continue to Loop B, but if walking Loop A only, we leave the turning point and follow the signpost back towards Kilcrohane. The going is now easy, a 3km (2-mile) walk along a quiet country road tracing the 150m contour, with spectacular views across to Beara. With the exception of summer weekends, there is almost no traffic. If the sky is blue, the waters of Bantry Bay glimmer and sparkle below us and the scene might be described as 'heavenly', especially in late summer and autumn when the gorse is laid out like golden carpets and the heather is at its brightest and best.

The lichens on the fence posts – sea ivory and *Xanathoria* – are luxuriant, and in the wet places we will see royal ferns. Cuckoo flowers thrive on the boggy land, pale pink and delicate, flowering from March to June, along with spectacular yellow flag-irises, bright yellow against the rushy ground where they thrive in midsummer. Stonechats perch on the tips of goat willows and a lark may be heard singing high above. In the heat of a summer day, the air is abuzz with bees and hoverflies, and butterflies dance along the ditches, speckled woods, ringlets and meadow browns, tortoiseshells, painted ladies and red admirals, all in their season.

Doo Lough

(6) Halfway along, 1.5km (1 mile) from the turning point, we begin to descend sharply and see a by-road leading to a farmhouse on our left. The steep descent continues beyond the turning. Coolturtaun Lough is clearly visible ahead and to our left, with a farm road skirting its eastern end. Farms dot the landscape; the terrain is becoming kinder as we walk eastwards. Soon, Laharandota Lough and the car park come into view.

On summer days, it is worth lingering a while and watching the lake. Damsel flies and demoiselles, lighter and slimmer than dragonflies, perch with their wings folded rather than splayed; they catch the sun and shine as if lacquered. Their flight is weaker and more fluttering than the darters or the true dragonflies (of the 'hawker' family), which perch with wings open wide. The emperor dragonfly, with a wingspan of over 10 cm (4 inches) and a body 7.5 cm (3 inches) long, first appeared in Ireland in 2008, and is annually expanding its range. An impressive creature, brilliant blue, green and silver, it hawks tirelessly over the lake surface, flying at up to 30 km/h (18 mph) in search of midges and flies.

LOOP B

(1) Parking at Tooreen turning point, we set off on the westernmost loop, the Sheep's Hoof, one might call it; it is, indeed, shaped somewhat like a hoof, with Lough Akeen splitting the 'toes'. The route is always spectacular but is quite arduous in places, especially difficult after successive days of rain.

We walk downhill on the track leading to the white house below on our left. Where the track forks, we take the upper path; there is a waymark ahead. Dunmanus Bay comes into view and the northern tip of Mizen, Three Castles Head. The path is rocky and may be mucky in the winter; as a result, footworn tracks sometimes skirt wet ground and return farther along.

Between April and October, we sometimes see wheatears on this route, wagtail-sized summer migrants. The electricity poles that march along the valleys to the lighthouse on the furthest tip somewhat mar the view of the broad Atlantic and impinge upon the unspoiled ruggedness of the world around us, much of which has never felt a human step.

Where pools collect after heavy rain, the walks committee has installed paving or stepping stones. As we proceed, we sometimes walk along valleys with rising ground on either side, with the panoramas temporarily obscured. However, this walk is replete with vistas. As we near the tip of the headland, we may climb a dozen steps above the path and find Lough Akeen directly below us. Care should be taken here: while it is the perfect location for Tarzan to swallow-dive straight down into the black depths, I imagine most walkers would prefer not to.

Beyond fingerpost 252, we head toward a gap with a makeshift road possibly used during the lighthouse construction – if we look back, a broad track can be detected, following the line of electricity poles.

From here, the beacon on Bere Island, marking the passage into Bere Haven, is very clear. Behind the hills on Beara are more hills, all the way back to Kerry, soft humps and contours fading into the distance.

(2) We reach a plateau and go fairly steeply downhill, the lake on our right, with reeds at the western end. Rectangular signs in distressed red paint announce 'Danger, Attention, Gefahr' (the recent signs, use 'Achtung' – Attention – instead) referring to the cliffs nearby. We cross a footbridge over a clear stream.

The path now takes us away from the cliffs; as we continue, we will see the jagged edge of a formidable precipice to our left. The tip of Beara is more and more visible as we proceed, the westernmost end of Dursey Island extending beyond Crow Head.

(3) Below us, we see a ring of stones painted white, a rudimentary helicopter pad, serving the lighthouse. A sign directs us to the lighthouse; painted in yellow, it is probably meant for helicopter crews arriving in the dark or in heavy fog to carry out emergency maintenance of the light. The structure was put in place by Gulf Oil to guide tankers into Bantry Bay to the Whiddy Island Oil Storage Depot. We can clearly make out its 'opposite number', the lighthouse on the Calf Rock off the tip of Dursey. Ships steering a course between the two would come safely into Bantry Bay, one of the largest deep-water harbours in Europe.

(4) We return to the helicopter pad and continue in the direction in which we've come before turning left towards a fingerpost below. We pass along a valley, passing Post 242 – we are doing this leg of the Sheep's Head Way anticlockwise.

The route next takes us through a shallow gorge like a small glaciated valley; however, glaciation is generally not considered to have reached these peninsulas. The valley continues for almost a kilometre; Irish butterwort, an insect-trapping 'carnivorous' plant with a beautiful flower in May and June, may be found in boggy places. The patterns and colours of lichens on the rocks cannot but make one pause; there are cobalt blues, deep and pastel greens, cadmium and egg-yolk yellows, red lichens and every shade of grey. Some (just before Post 239) are snow-white, big blobs, almost like white paint.

In all but the driest summers, we come on wet patches, over which we must tread softly. Now, more signs of danger and we pass close to a cliff edge with drops of 60 m (200ft) into the sea. A small length of guardrail has been erected.

(5) At roughly this point, we can see, far below us, a smooth rock, shiny and grey, showing just above the surface between the swells; one is immediately reminded of the back of a humpbacked whale. James O'Mahony – local historian, part-time farmer and Rural Recreation officer for the Sheep's Head Way – told me that, long ago, it was a renowned mark for catching gilthead sea bream with rod and line. These fish, which disappeared almost overnight, were a staple in the diet of the Sheep's Head people, and were salted, dried and traded. They may have even reached Newfoundland where the western sea bream is known as 'the sheepshead'. Is it possible that ships leaving Bantry Bay for America took stocks of salt bream from Muntervary with them to be eaten on the voyage?

Now, on a cliff face on our left, fulmar can be seen gliding on the air currents or sitting on their nests in grassy niches. The feature now is the cliffs and the views of Beara. Passing Post 236, we reach a stile over a fence, and start up a slope on the left-hand side, following the posts. On a humpbacked salient near 235, we must be careful not to totter over an inland cliff and fall many feet onto the gorse and heather below.

(6) At Post 231, a map of the entire Sheep's Head route is displayed and it is here that we turn right, following the waymarks steeply uphill to complete the loop, while the 'main' track continues east towards Bantry. Some distance up this rough slope, we come to a galvanised gate with a stile beside it and some stepping stones just beyond.

Butterwort with bugs

Sheep's Head and Beara sunset   *Sheep's Head in September*

At the top of the first ridge, we can see, eastwards, what appear to be two standing stones but are, in fact, the gables of a roofless stone house, with rough fields marked by stone walls in front of it. This is the first indication of settlement. We continue to the second ridge, topped by electricity poles marching westwards. We come upon a low stone wall and a stream, with foxgloves, celandine and St Patrick's Cabbage established in the shelter along its sides.

Now, there are rough fields, the stones cleared from them thrown on the boundary ditches, and a roofless stone ruin. Below, on a ditch, a wind-sculpted tree, probably a *sceac* (blackthorn), has managed to grow. The ascending track we follow was once the path into this smallholding and may have been walked for centuries. It climbs alongside walls increasingly colonised by saxifrage and ferns, and there are a few fields. Shortly afterwards, we see the electricity poles again and then Tooreen turning point above us, where we may finish our walk or pause for refreshment before, perhaps, continuing to Loop A.

GLENGARRIFF WOODS NATURE RESERVE

Key points: Ireland's second largest native oak forest — panoramic views over forest and mountains — woodland and riverside walks — moorland, meadow and bog — rare flora and fauna.

Start/finish: Glengarriff Woods Nature Reserve car park, grid ref. V927563

Distance: 6.5km (4 miles)
Map: OSi Sheet 85 **Walking Time:** 2 hours 30 minutes

At the western end of Glengarriff village, the road forks at the graveyard. We take the right fork, signposted Kenmare. We continue to the big gates at the entrance of Glengarriff Nature Reserve and walk or drive to the car park, where there are picnic tables and information boards describing the flora and fauna we will encounter on our trail through these magnificent oak woodlands.

(1) From the car park, we return towards the gate and follow signs for Lady Bantry's Walk, the first leg of our itinerary. We cross the river via a stone bridge and soon begin to ascend a fairly steep path with occasional steps, once an ancient track continuing to the far reaches of Beara. We ignore a path to our right going to the Big Meadow Walk.

(2) Soon we cross a tarred a road and continue up the narrow stone steps on the other side to Lady Bantry's lookout. The vegetation alongside the steps is a typical understorey mix of holly, hazel and willow. There are whortleberry bushes nearby: they bear pinkish-white flowers and small, dark blue berries in summer, called 'hurts' or *fraughan*, from the Irish. In the past, they were gathered on Fraughan Sunday, the last Sunday in July, and at *Lúnasa* in August. An example grows to the left of the metal post that says 'Nature Reserve'.

Close to the ground, hard ferns and tormentil grow prolifically.

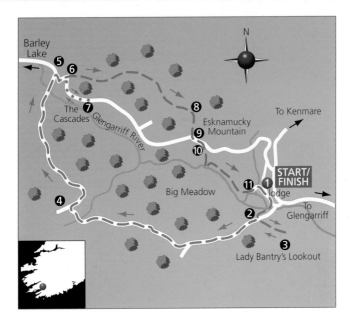

The trunks of the oaks are mossy: some are dead but still standing. Channels cross the path to take away winter rain and some of the steps are formed by tree roots. Some of the rocks on the right may support St Patrick's Cabbage, a saxifrage that is one of Ireland's unique Lusitanian species.

(3) After the final flight of steps, we emerge from the trees onto the summit and a breathtaking view over Glengarriff. Bare outcrops of rock crown the summit and two seats overlook the panorama. Below us we see the western spur of Bantry Bay, Glengarriff Harbour, with the vast bay itself farther to the right. At the centre of the harbour is the islet of Garvillaun, almost joined to Ilnacullin, known locally as Garinish Island. We can see part of Garinish, renowned for its gardens, which flourish in the unique microclimate of the harbour and are enjoyed by many thousands of visitors each year. The top of the Martello tower

The Glengarriff River

is visible above the shelter belt of pines that ring the shore. Almost opposite us, due east in the mainland woods, a white house can be seen amongst the trees, and to the right of it a castle, Dromgarriff, a long-abandoned castellated house with towers at either end, now blending with the surrounding forest. The spur of the bay in front is crossed by mussel lines: mussel farming is a local industry.

Behind us, we can see the full extent of the woodlands, which all but fill Glengarriff glen beneath the bare slopes of the Caha Mountains. Here and there, rock faces show between the dense canopy of the ancient sessile oak forests, second in importance only to Killarney oak woods. From this high lookout, we can see that oak covers 70 per cent or more of the 300 hectares of the National Park, with stands of pine amongst them. Looking north, to the mountains, we may see the Tunnel Road to Kenmare. The sandstone slopes of the Caha range continue west, the land terraced by folding and glaciation, with levels of rough grass in between.

As we turn from the view and start down the steps, we might look out for an example of another Hiberno-Lusitanian species, the arbutus or strawberry tree, on the left just below the summit. In autumn, the fruits are strawberry colour but resemble tiny, bumpy-skinned oranges. They are sweet but have a strange texture and many seeds. Ancient pollen traces show that arbutus grew in Irish oak woods 2,000 years ago. Some of the present trees may be direct descendants. Typically found on forest edges, they thrive when fire or human agency lets light into the forest. The trunks are favoured by a harmless Lusitanian invertebrate, the False Scorpion, at least for moulting and reproduction.

Arriving back on the road below, we turn left, walking through dappled shade under oak trees, the leaves of the holly gleaming like silver in the semi-darkness where they catch the sun. Green-veined White butterflies and the smaller Wood White, a rare species, may be seen. Here and there the road is skirted by attractive, silver-trunked birch trees. The squawk of a jay may be heard and the flash of its iridescent blue wings glimpsed through the trees. They are very handsome crows with a taste for acorns: oak woods are their favourite habitat in Ireland.

On the right, we pass two black bollards at the start of a trail but we continue on the road. There is no traffic whatsoever, even on busy weekends, so it is as pleasant as walking a forest track, possibly better because it is more open, and dry in winter. The holly trees, some as tall as 10m (33ft), line the route with silver on sunny days. A small stream runs by the roadside. We cross a bridge with walls of plain concrete

Glengarriff Harbour and Garvillaun

blocks. The road is fringed by goat willow, the upright-standing catkins like furry bottle brushes in May, green if they are female, golden if male. The name may arise from that fact that, in the past, they were coppiced so that goats could graze the new shoots.

We briefly leave the cover of the trees and pass a wooden gate and stile signposted Big Meadow Walk – we continue on the road. A by-road leads into a house. We are going downhill, the land falling away steeply on our right and rising above the road on the left. The road is attractive, dappled with light and shadow, with tall birches, occasional beech trees and oaks overhead, sphagnum and moss on the ditches. We pass a stand of tall pines, like a corner of Transylvania, and then a bungalow with neat lawns. We cross the pretty Coomarkane river via a concrete bridge. We can see the high slopes of the hills above the trees.

(4) We turn right opposite a sign for the Bantry Cycle Path, sharp right, almost back on ourselves. Grass grows down the middle of this road, which is fringed with pines. Ahead and above, we can again see traffic climbing the winding road up to the tunnels. To the left, there

A typical quiet road in Glengarriff

are striking grass terraces amongst the slabs and outcrops of weather-worn rock, with occasional rivulets running down them, catching the sun. Topping the rise, we see Esk Mountain, one of the Cahas, straight ahead, with the spruce plantations giving out at a certain height to be replaced by brakes of French gorse, very golden on the mountainside in May. Season to season, some of the land around is sere or dark green, depending on the volume of rainfall. Now, we see occasional stands of rhododendron, ominous because it is so invasive and destructive to native plants. We also notice low-growing bog myrtle which, in terms of habitat, would define this piece of wetland as a forest. Amongst the myrtle, bog cotton flowers into white tufts in spring. On the low hill beyond the bog, there has been extensive tree felling. Otherwise, this is wild country, with minimal human interference.

The dormers of a house deep in the woods ahead may be noticed but it is almost lost amongst the trees. Even on sunny, summer Sundays this is a quiet road, an idyll for walkers. As we round a corner, we see a fine Scots pine on the left with, typically, the red-barked trunk bare until it reaches the crown, often flattened, high above. Our only indigenous pine, they were once as 'native' as the oaks. However, the last 'original' Scots pine in Ireland died in 1866 and those we see now are the descendants of trees brought from the Scottish Highlands. Some experts believe the species originated here and migrated to Scotland via the pre-Ice Age land bridge.

The route downhill is very steep. We cross a second concrete bridge over a small river, the Glengarriff River, which we will join again farther downstream.

(5) Arriving at a T-junction, we go right (a sign points left to Barley Lake). This is a continuation of the Beara Way Cycle Path with which our route coincided as we came downhill. We are on a wider road now.

(6) We shortly pass an ivy-grown stone house and reach a corner with a black-and-amber barrier across a forest path and a wooden wicket beside it. We will take this path but, first, it is worthwhile walking a little farther on the road to the car park just beyond.

(7) Beside it, are The Cascades, small waterfalls and a large pool where families picnic and swim in summer. Returning to the forest path mentioned above, we pass through the wicket and set off down the

The Cascades on a summer Sunday

green lane. Young birches grow alongside: the shiny bark is chestnut red, not silver at first. The bark of the ubiquitous goat willows is grey. As we walk, only birdsong punctuates the almost perfect silence and our only company is likely to be the speckled wood butterflies that flit amongst the trees or, at dusk, bats careering overhead, turning and flying back at us, hair-raisingly low. Seven species of bat occur around Glengarriff, the most important of which is the Lesser Horseshoe bat. Extinct in many parts of Europe, they typically forage along woodland rides.

We pass impressively tall oaks, beeches and birches. We ignore a narrow, footworn path to the left. Looking right, we see dramatic hills, with slabs of exposed bedrock and rivers of green between them. The path is fringed with foxgloves, blue 'hazes' of forget-me-nots on the grassy verge and club moss in wet spots. A fingerpost, with the outline of a green walker on it, points the way we have come and, here, a track goes right but we ignore it.

(8) Reaching a Y, we take the right fork, going downhill slightly. The Esknamucky Walk climbs the hill to the left. Known as the High Walk, it presents panoramic views over the forest and hills. We pass a small

pond on the left, and pass between two stone gateposts. There is a path to the left (this is, actually, the usual route of the Esknamucky Walk but is sometimes closed for tree-felling). We go straight ahead, downhill, on a green path, and step onto the road via a wooden stile.

(9) We turn left here. Care should be taken: this road may have some traffic.

However, we shortly leave it at a substantial wooden gate on the right (10), setting off down the pleasant green track beyond. Passing a big, boggy field on our right, colonised with rushes and pinkish-purple cuckoo flowers in spring, we reach a Y-junction (11) where the track curves left. Here, we go straight ahead on a narrower path. Almost immediately, we see a bridge with steps up to it. A nearby sign says Big Meadow Walk; this continues on the other side of the bridge.

Our route does not cross the bridge, but goes left on a pretty flagstone path along the river. However, it is worthwhile stepping onto the bridge and leaning on the parapet, looking downstream. These rivers contain trout and salmon, the gravelled shallows providing ideal conditions for spawning. Almost beneath the bridge on the left, a robust carpet of St Patrick's Cabbage has colonised the seemingly bare rock and blooms in a haze of pink flowers in late spring.

Taking up the well-made path along the river, we soon reach a wooden bridge over a small tributary. Here, we turn right at a big spreading oak, and follow the river. We pass a picturesque pool with seats alongside it, then a yellow post with a lifebuoy attached and a path to a small, gravel river-beach – people swim all along this stretch of water. Inside the gravelled path, a footworn route stays closer to the river but soon emerges onto the gravel. This is a classic riverside walk, light and shade on the clear water, dark, still pools, and small, murmuring cascades. Here and there, brakes of yellow broom light up the dark foliage along the mossy fern-grown banks. The air is almost misty, cool even in the heat of summer.

The path divides at a mighty oak with twelve or more great limbs spreading from the trunk into the crown. We can go left or right of it. Beneath, hazel and holly thrive in the shadow of the huge canopy. On the river bank, tall meadow buttercups grow riotously amongst the stands of dark bluebells, their lacquered yellow petals catching the sun. Crossing a small wooden bridge over a tributary we shortly arrive at the car park where we began.

BERE ISLAND WALK

Key points: Nineteenth-century school – Martello tower – standing stone – rugged scenery

Start/finish: West Pier on Bere Island, where the ferry arrives, grid ref.: V685446

Distance: 9km (5.5 miles)
Map: OSi Sheet 84 **Walking time:** 2 hours

Bere Island lies on the northwest side of Bantry Bay, off the fishing port of Castletownberehaven. It is reached by ferries from the town quays (fifteen minutes), and from Pontoon (twenty minutes), off the R572 about 4km (2.4 miles) east of the town. The island is 11km (7 miles) long, by 5km (3 miles) wide, at widest point, and rises to 258m (846ft). It has a population of 210 at the time of writing. There is a shop, two pubs, a post office, a restaurant, a B&B and two hostels. There are some good coves for swimming. Ted O'Sullivan's *Bere Island, a Short History* supplied useful material for this walk.

Our route follows a section of the Beara Way, of which the island can boast some of the loveliest stretches. The scenery is magnificent and a feature is the profusion of wild flowers.

As we cross in the ferry, we may contemplate the ruins of Dunboy Castle, on the mainland to the southwest, the shell of a once-fine house of many windows, now stark and empty, the walls and casements ivy-grown. This was the last home of Donal Cam O'Sullivan Beare, the last lord of Beara, who paid the price for his support of the Irish cause at Kinsale in 1601 when the victorious English general, Carew, marched west, burning and levelling all remaining pockets of Irish resistance. So it was with Dunboy. Carew and his regiments approached the castle from Bere Island, and after a siege of eleven days left it in ruins, having slaughtered all within. O'Sullivan fled to Dursey and, after it too was overrun and its people massacred, set off on the bitter march to Leitrim, briefly recounted in the Dursey Island Walk.

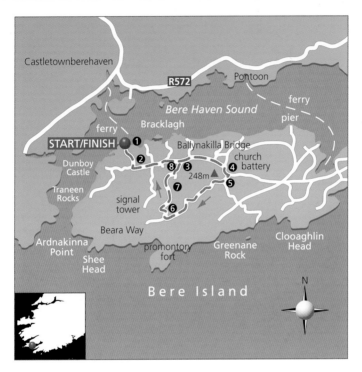

(1) We begin the walk at the West Pier. Some of the parked cars are falling to pieces where they stand and these, along with a couple of wrecked boats, make the scene picturesque and distinctly not 'mainland'. Nearby, is a modern cafe serving Italian coffee and light meals. There are signs for the Beara Way and Cycle Route.

The road up from the pier is delightfully old-fashioned, the ditches being host to every common wild flower as it comes into season, and to fuchsia, gorse and heather too. All the island ditches are similarly rich in blooms and blossoms; perhaps they have never been subjected to the pesticides or flail saws that mainland road verges suffer annually and as a result, burgeon with flowers and wild shrubs, some seldom seen on the mainland, and a delight to the eye. We pass between

Old farmhouse with Maulin and Knockagree Mountains across the strait

well-kept houses, with gardens, a shed with a red corrugated roof and a pretty cottage. A ruined signal tower is silhouetted on the hill ahead of us, another of the chain of towers built by the English along the southwest coast as an early-warning system against a repeat of the attempted French invasion of 1798. Stone walls climb the hill, seemingly dividing fallow land from fallow land to little purpose. Perhaps they were part of Famine Relief schemes set in place to insure the Irish would earn whatever little help they got.

(2) We arrive at a T-junction and turn left, in the Rerrin direction, also signposted for the Beara Way. We pass a Marian shrine, built in 1954, and from the high ground soon get panoramic views of Castletownbere across the channel. There is a standing stone and house ruins in the fields to the right.

The road is tarred, and undulating, with little or no traffic, rising on the right, falling away to the sea on the left. Trees surround the houses, as shelter belts. We ignore the crossroads, and continue on the straight road east. For a short distance, pines grow on both sides of the road, and then there are fields with gorse and heather, resplendent in late summer. We ignore the turning down to the left and pass fields grazed by sheep before passing the new school, built in 1980, on the left, its perimeter wall painted by the children with scenes from Irish legends. There is a pretty ruin beside it, an old cottage with a rusting, red corrugated roof.

We now see a sign to the left for Ballynakilla and, after crossing Ballynakilla Bridge, we pass the old school – a site with marvellous views – its yard overgrown with rushes, loosestrife, royal fern, montbretia, field scabious, bindweed and a dozen other wild flowers. On the wall to the right of the gate, a sign tells us that in 1828, there were three schools on Bere Island, the Ballynakilla school being a mud cabin with one teacher and 97 pupils. It was replaced by this building in 1857; in 1928, it still had 100 pupils, dropping to 39 by 1980, when it was replaced by the new school.

Pupil numbers reflect the decline in population on Bere Island. Pre-Famine, in 1841, it was 2,122; ten years later, it was 1,454. It plunged again when the market for fish collapsed and went into steeper decline after the Second World War. It has stabilised since the millennium and now numbers about 210 residents.

In autumn, the hedges stretching beyond the school are purple with fuchsia, and golden with dwarf gorse and lady's bedstraw – the Bere Island roads could accurately be called Wild Flower Walks. Montbretia still blooms in early September, when it is largely gone on the mainland, and the dwarf gorse is in its first flowering, a lovely sight.

(3) We ignore the right turning, climbing the hill and go straight ahead. We have spectacular views of the Slieve Miskish Mountains across the sound; we are opposite Maulin and Knocknagree, with Hungry Hill to the right. The folds are especially striking in evening light, when they are defined by deep shadows. An abandoned house, with twin chimneys, stands between us and the channel.

Now, as we top a rise on the road, there's a pub – roofless, at the time of writing – on the right, and a Martello tower on a bare hill ahead of us. We ignore the left turning marked Rerrin and the Beara Cycle Route; Greenane is signposted ahead and there is a roadside map of the island, erected by the Irish Heart Foundation. Pines line the road, with occasionally large trees, sycamore and ash. We ignore another left. The road rises relatively steeply; we can see that it levels off ahead. Unfortunately, there is stand of Japanese knotweed along here on the left; it should be eradicated (if that is possible) before it begins to subsume the marvellous local flora.

(4) Amongst a nest of roadside signs, a sign directs us right for the Bere Island standing stone and the lighthouse. We take this and walk uphill now. We will shortly see the standing stone, or *gallán*, on our left, with a Heritage Plaque telling us that it dates from the Bronze Age, 2000 BC to 500 BC, time of the legendary Tuatha de Danann, and that it is said to mark the exact centre of the island. We are now up very high, and get magnificent views of the standing stone, the Martello tower and the huge bulk of Hungry Hill across the water. On the lower slopes, the hill wears a skirt of green. We can see another tower at the eastern end of Bere and, looking across Bantry Bay, the big caves and coves on the southern shore and the tip of the Sheep's Head protruding far into the Atlantic.

(5) Opposite the standing stone, we leave the road and take the hill track. A sign tells us this section of the Beara Way is closed on 31 January each year; no doubt the landowner wishes to assert his rights over the route. A stile gives access. No dogs are allowed; there are sheep loose on the hillside. We can see a cross on the small hill ahead.

The track curves around; there is nothing but rush and dwarf gorse. The higher we go, the better the views, and it is breathtaking to look down on the world below. At the cross, erected in 1950 to commemorate the Holy Year, we look back and see that there are two small lakes almost between us and the Martello tower. Shortly afterwards, we reach the top of our gentle climb, and start down. We can no longer see the Sheep's Head; we are looking straight out into the Atlantic where an Air India flight so tragically went down in 1985, blown out of the sky by a terrorist bomb, with a loss of all 329 lives aboard it.

The scenery is wild and rugged, of rock and bog; there is no sign of a house or of a human being. Bird life is scarce too, mainly ravens and rock pipits, but kestrels and peregrine falcons may be seen too. The ruined signal tower we saw from the pier is now on a hill ahead of us, and we can see all the way up the coast to Black Ball Head (also with a signal tower) and to White Ball Head, with a promontory fort, beyond. The track is good, wide enough for a off-road vehicle. As we start to descend, we have as fine a view of Castletownbere as one could wish for.

Bere Island house, with windows facing inland

Colourful wrecked van

(6) The path reaches a T-junction, and we go right. White, daisy-like camomile edges the path in places, still flowering late in the year. We are heading downhill towards the Bere Haven Sound, back to civilisation, the island houses and the town across the water. We pass some pines and reach a surfaced road.

(7) Now, to the left, is the continuance of the Beara Way, taking the walker to the west end of the island and then back to the pier; this option can be easily followed on the OS map and would add about 4km (2.4 miles) to our walk. However, we ignore the track and continue on the road, passing white gates and a white farmhouse, heading down to Ballynakilla Bridge. The road rises slightly, little used, with grass growing up the middle.

(8) We reach the dorsal road again at Ballynakilla Bridge, and turn left, walking west to the turning that takes us down to the pier and the ferry to the mainland. It is a short but pleasant voyage, especially on a summer evening with the sun setting behind Slieve Miskish and mackerel breaking the water around the boat.

DURSEY ISLAND WALK

Key points: Ireland's only cable car – ruined abbey – abandoned hamlets – Bull Rock lighthouse – views north to Kerry – ridge walk, heather gorse and sheep

Start/finish: the cable-car landing place on Dursey, grid ref.: V505416

***

Distance: 20km (12 miles)
Map: OSi Sheet 84 **Walking Time:** 4 to 5 hours

***

Dursey Island lies at the extreme western end of the Beara Peninsula, 24km beyond Castletownbere. Above Ballaghboy Pier (grid ref. 508418), a cable car crosses the Sound to the island, which is 6.4 km (4 miles) long, and a maximum of 2.4km (1.5 miles) wide. It rises to 251m (825ft) at the highest point of the dorsal ridge that runs from east to west. On the south side of the ridge, there are three small settlements; the island's fields are clustered around or between these. The north side of the ridge slopes more steeply to the sea, a landscape of bracken, gorse and heather which is grazed by sheep and goats but offers little shelter or pasture. There is no shop, overnight accommodation or public phone on Dursey. There is a post box; mail is collected and taken to the cable car.

I am privileged to have Penny Durell's *Discover Dursey* to hand, a small volume replete with information.

Dursey is different from the relatively sheltered islands of Roaringwater and Bantry Bay. There are no hedgerow-skirted lanes and no wild trees, although some cottages have small shelter belts of shrubs, sycamore and low pines. It is a high island and affords marvellous walking, with traffic-less roads and unfenced hills. The views are always memorable, with bird's-eye prospects of the island below us, of the blue mountains of Kerry across the expanse of the Kenmare River – actually an enormous bay –or south, across Bantry Bay, to the finger of hills that is the Sheep's Head peninsula.

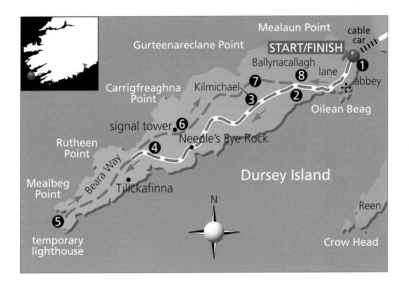

Dursey is spectacular in a bare, ascetic way. In winter, the landscape is brown and sere, and the sea grey beneath its steep cliffs and coves. It is romantic when curtains of soft rain blow across the small green fields and ruined cottages. It is sun-baked in good summers, for there are no trees, and no shade. It is loveliest of all in September, when our native gorse is in flower and its rolling hills are dressed in brilliant gold, dramatic against the deep blue of the sea.

But for all its beauty, Dursey has a tragic history. In 1602, after the Irish defeat at Kinsale, its 300 inhabitants, members of the O'Sullivan clan, were massacred, and all of Beara was put to fire and sword. Finally, in the freezing winter of that year, the chieftain, Donal Cam O'Sullivan Beare, led what was left of his people on a long ghost-march to refuge with their O'Rourke kinsmen in far-off Leitrim, harried and attacked by both English and Irish every mile of the way. Of the 1,000 men women and children who set out, only 35 reached their destination.

We cross to Dursey by Ireland's only cable car, operated by Cork

Setting out . . .

County Council, and traverse the abyss between the headland and the island in a stout box carrying six passengers suspended some 26m (80ft) above the sea. A new car came into operation in late 2009. The old car now rests in a local farmyard, serving as a henhouse. A range of poultry, including fine turkey cocks and geese, share the enclosure, and spectacular peacocks roam free. A life-size fibreglass lamb stands in the doorway of the car, a reminder of the fact that these transports of delights traditionally carry not only passengers but livestock, including sheep and cattle, to the island.

(1) We set off from the cable-car landing place; the car was installed in 1969, inspired by a local man who had rigged up a pulley to transfer his sheep across the abyss. The landing place is known as *Áit an Fheoir*, 'the site of the massacre'. Here, in June 1602, Carew's soldiers paraded children pinioned on their spears, shot and hacked islanders to death and roped others together in groups and pushed them over the cliffs into the sea.

The open road ahead rises gently. In September, with the gorse in bloom, it crosses a landscape of gold. A path runs down to the left, to the pier. Until the cable car, this was the point of access but in winter months it was often cut off for days or weeks at a time.

Now, below us on the left we clearly see the monastery and burial ground, once known as St Mary's Abbey, perched above the sea. Philip O'Sullivan Beare, born on Dursey, wrote of the island during his long exile in Spain where he was a foremost scholar and a commander of the navy. He relates that the monastery was founded by one Bonaventure, a Spanish bishop who held the See of Ross, but it is likely that a much earlier chapel existed on the site.

The *Oileán Beag* is dramatically separated from Dursey by a steep-sided channel, once spanned by a drawbridge. A castle and fortifications were installed by Philip O'Sullivan's father, Diarmuid, in the late sixteenth century. Carew's forces levelled these in 1602, and the defenders and civilians who had taken refuge there were slaughtered.

The road is unfenced, with grass growing down the middle. We pass a parking space where islanders leave their cars when they take the cable car to Ireland. Dursey casts a spell from the moment one arrives. We are in a dimension removed from the everyday world. Topping the rise, we see the signal tower on the island's highest hill: it is a constant presence, silhouetted against the sky.

Dursey cottage

St Mary's Abbey

Sheep on the cliff

(2) The road climbs steeply to the hamlet of Ballynacallagh, a dozen or so houses, some renovated, some in ruins, and small outhouses with tin roofs painted red. The house clusters on Dursey are all attractive. The houses are almost all the same, single storey but tall, with steeply pitched slate roofs and chimneys at either end. Happily, restorations have not changed their character. They are, largely, grey, built of stone and melding into the landscape; some are whitewashed, in the old tradition.

Beyond the hamlet, we pass the island postbox, somewhat rusted, and walk downhill, passing small fields divided by stone walls. Ahead, we see the settlement of Kilmichael. Ruins on the hillside above us include the school.

(3) At Kilmichael, free-range chickens scratch along the roadside. About 1km (0.6 miles) beyond the village, a turf-cutter's road goes up to the right. We will meet this in the highlands later. We round a bend and soon pass through a gate. The road now narrows, with a cliff face on one side and a hair-raising drop to the sea on the other. Rocks, fallen from above, lie against the cliff on our right. One rock is split, forming a narrow passage. Legend had it that if a newly wed girl

passed through the fissure of the Needle's Eye Rock three times from east to west, she would not die in childbirth.

Soon, we can see, far off, the stump of the lighthouse on the Calf Rock, at the western end. We pass fields enclosed by stone walls (the stones were cleared from the fields, so the walls were dual-purpose) running, in parallel, down to the shore.

(4) Tilickafinna hamlet, which we pass through next, has a scatter of some six houses, all facing south, a few renovated.

We pass through a gap in a stone wall and, leaving the last house on the island behind, we go through a gate onto a green road curving gracefully uphill and taking us to a scalp from which we look down on the green sward of the western headland, grazed by sheep. The views are magnificent, Iveragh with the Ring of Kerry, to the north, blue mountains behind blue mountains and, offshore, Scariff and Deenish islands, the one green and humpbacked like the Great Blasket, the other bare and angular like Small Skellig. Near in, to the north, are the Cow and then the Bull Rock, with its gleaming lighthouse. Through binoculars, both seem almost clouded in birds; indeed, they are amongst the ten most important coastal bird sites in Ireland, the Bull Rock being Ireland's second largest gannetry, with over 1,500 breeding pairs, while both islands host breeding storm petrels, guillemot, razorbill, fulmar and other species. Here on the headlands, we may also enjoy the sight of choughs soaring and tumbling overhead, with black glossy feathers and red beaks and legs, and peregrine falcons may be seen here too.

(5) Foot-worn paths now take us over the headland's crown and down a steep slope to the temporary lighthouse which, after the sea destroyed the Calf Rock light in 1881, warned off shipping until the Bull Rock lighthouse was completed. The Calf, the Cow and the Bull have long been a danger to seafarers. Waves have been seen to engulf the Cow entirely, which stands 64m (205ft) above the sea. Such waves took away the top of the cast iron tower on the Calf Rock light in November 1881, forcing the three keepers and three workmen to flee to a concrete bunker where, for twelve days, they were trapped in a tiny space, the sea raging over them. Numerous attempts to reach them were defeated by the strength of the storms.

Weather permitting, this western end of Dursey is a fine spot to perch for an hour and contemplate the western ocean. Maritime history is close by, above the waves and beneath them. Even on halcyon days, there is often a small breeze while, out of the wind, it can be as warm as the Mediterranean. No cars, no sound; white waves breaking in silent animation on black rocks under the Bull light. Far below us, squadrons of gannets fly over the stiff, blue sea.

(6) With splendid views of sea, islands and distant mountains, we turn and begin the return leg of our walk. Our landmark, now, is the signal tower silhouetted on top of *Cnoc Mór* ('the big hill'), to the east. The Beara Way markers guide us to a path meandering up to the summit at 252m (819ft). Penny Durrell reports that islanders would light bonfires here to bid farewell to sons or daughters passing on emigrant ships to America. The tower was started in 1804, and possibly never completed. It was part of a chain of towers, each visible from the one before and after, built along the coast in response to English fears of a more determined French incursion than that of 1796 into Bantry Bay.

The views are outstanding. Bantry Bay opens to the south, with Sheep's Head and the Mizen Head, beyond. Northwards, in clear weather we may see the Skellig Rocks, redoubt of the early Irish church, off the coast of Kerry; even the distant Blaskets may be seen on a fine day. The island itself is laid out below us.

The tower and deserted village

A peacock near Ballaghboy Pier with Dursey in the background

Beyond the tower, our route starts downhill. There is evidence of turf-cutting. We cross a wide track, running from the south shore to the north, where there is a *fulacht fiadh* site, a Bronze Age cooking place. Following the Beara Way (at waymark No. 66, a stile) we reach a lag between the hills and some flat, boggy ground. From here, we can see the white swathe of Ballydonegan Strand and Allihies on the mainland. The waymarked path climbs again, skirting the next low hill on its northern side.

(7) On the descent, we encounter a steep slope for 50m (56 yards) or so, the houses of Kilmichael below us on the right. We arrive at a track running along a stone wall; it goes right to Kilmichael but we go left, crossing a bridge over a narrow stream. We meet a stone wall beautifully colonised by white lichens, with sheep wire on top (waymark No. 72). A stile bridges this. The route takes us around a corner of the wall and we are on a green path, part of the old bog road to the turf cuttings (waymark No. 75). The high ground is now on our left; between us and the sea are fields with cattle. Butterflies, especially Small Heaths, Meadow Browns and Ringlets are abundant here, but they are everywhere on the island. Pied wagtails are also a feature and swallows in summer, using Kilmichael's ruins for nesting places.

(8) The path swings sharply right, descending to a gate. Passing through it, we are walking down a lane, into Ballynacallagh village. On the stone walls, bell heather and ling thrive (the ling is pink, the heather, purple) along with wall rue, stone crop, foxgloves and fuchsia; there is Japanese knotweed in a garden, perhaps once sown as a decorative plant but now, as usual, subsuming all other growth. At the T-junction, we meet the road, and go left for the cable car.

Ferry and Cable-car Timetables

All sailings subject to weather and other conditions

Bere Island Ferry
Daily Timetable

21 June – 22 September				22 September – 20 June			
Depart Castletown		Depart Bere Island		Depart Castletown		Depart Bere Island	
Mon–Sat	Sun	Mon–Sat	Sun	Mon–Sat	Sun	Mon–Sat	Sun
0800*	1230	0745*	1200	0800*	1230	0745*	1200
0900	1500	0830	1430	0900	1700	0830	1630
1130	1700	1000	1630	1130	1900	1000	1830
1330	1900	1230	1830	1330		1245	
1530	2000	1430	1930	1615		1515	
1730		1630		1830		1800	
1830		1800		2030 (Fri only)		2000 (Fri only)	
2030		2000					

www.bereislandferries.com   * except Saturdays and Bank Holidays

Cape Clear Island Ferry
Daily Timetable

		From Baltimore	From Cape
May & Sept	Mon–Sat	1030, 1400, 1800	0900, 1200, 1630
	Sun	1100, 1400, 1800	1000, 1200, 1700
June	Mon–Sat	1030, 1400, 1800	0900, 1200, 1630
	Sun	1100, 1400, 1700, 1900	1000, 1200, 1600, 1800
	Fridays only	0800	1900
July & August	Mon–Sat	1030, 1400, 1700, 1900	0900, 1200, 1600, 1800
	Sun	1100, 1400, 1700, 1900	1000, 1200, 16,00, 1800
October to April	Check website for details.		

www.cailinoir.com

Dursey Cable Car

Summer: the cable car runs continuously from 0900 to 2000.

Winter: 0930–1030; 1430–1630; 1900–1930. Sundays: 0900–1000; 1300–1400; 1900–1930.

For information, call: 00353 (0) 27 70054

Long Island Ferry

April–October		November–March	
Depart Colla Pier, Schull	Depart Long Island	Depart Colla Pier, Schull	Depart Long Island
0845	0900	0945	1000
0945*	1000*	1545	1600
1545*	1600*	No weekend scheduled services in winter	
1645	1700		

All sailings Monday, Wednesday and Friday except * which are Saturday and Sunday only.

The water taxi service is available at all other times at reasonable notice. Contact the operator at 086 172 1254 for enquiries and bookings.

Baltimore to Sherkin Island Ferry

Ferries for Sherkin Island leave from the small fishing village of Baltimore (trip takes approx. ten minutes) and also from Cunnamore Pier, on the Schull side of Skibbereen, (trip takes approx. fifteen minutes).

July/August

Depart Baltimore

0745*, 0900**, 1030, 1200, 1300, 1400, 1500, 1600, 1645, 1730, 1900, 2030

Depart Sherkin

0800*, 0945**, 1045, 1215, 1315, 1415, 1515, 1615, 1700, 1745, 1915, 2045

* Excluding Saturdays and Sundays
** Excluding Sundays

Ferries run many times daily throughout the year, phone 087 263 8470 / 087 244 7828 / 087 911 7377; or to receive a timetable, send a text message for the day you are enquiring about to 085 887 7422 (e.g. send word **Tuesday** to get timetable for Tuesday).

www.sherkinisland.eu

Also from The Collins Press

Carrauntoohil & MacGillycuddy's Reeks
A Walking Guide to Ireland's Highest Mountains
Jim Ryan

CONNEMARA & MAYO
Mountains, Coastal & Island Walks
A Walking Guide
Paul Phelan

THE DINGLE, IVERAGH & BEARA PENINSULAS
A Walking Guide
Adrian Hendroff

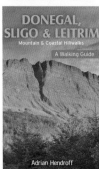

DONEGAL, SLIGO & LEITRIM
Mountain & Coastal Hillwalks
A Walking Guide
Adrian Hendroff

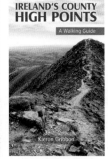

IRELAND'S COUNTY HIGH POINTS
A Walking Guide
Kieron Gribbon

A GUIDE TO IRELAND'S MOUNTAIN SUMMITS
THE VANDELEUR-LYNAMS & THE ARDERINS

NORTHERN IRELAND
A Walking Guide
Helen Fairbairn

PILGRIM PATHS IN IRELAND
From Slieve Mish to Skellig Michael
A Guide
John G. O'Dwyer

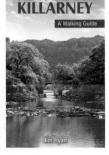

SCENIC WALKS IN KILLARNEY
A Walking Guide
Jim Ryan

The Burren & The Aran Islands
A Walking Guide
Tony Kirby

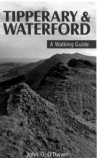

TIPPERARY & WATERFORD
A Walking Guide
John G. O'Dwyer